The Case for Black Reparations

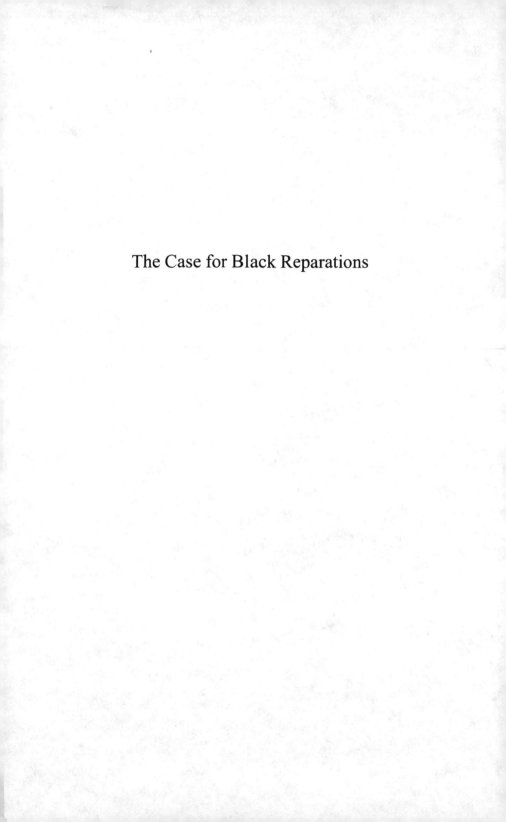

The Case for
Black Reparations

Boris I. Bittker

Beacon Press
Boston

Beacon Press
25 Beacon Street
Boston, Massachusetts 02108-2892
www.beacon.org

Beacon Press books
are published under the auspices of
the Unitarian Universalist Association of Congregations.

07 06 05 04 03 8 7 6 5 4 3 2 1

This book is printed on acid-free paper
that meets the uncoated paper ANSI/NISO
specifications for permanence as revised in 1992.

Library of Congress Cataloging-in-Publication Data
Bittker, Boris I.
The case for Black reparations / Boris I. Bittker.
p. cm.
Originally published: New York : Random House, 1973.
Includes bibliographical references.
ISBN 0-8070-0981-4 (alk. paper)
1. Slavery—Law and legislation—United States—History.
2. Afro-Americans—Legal status, laws, etc.—United States.
3. Restitution—United States. 4. United States—Claims.   I. Title.
KF4757.B58 2003
342.73´0873—dc21
2003043731

In Memoriam
Martin Luther King, Jr.

Contents

Foreword

Drew S. Days III

Black reparations was a subject of much debate and controversy in the early 1960s. At that time, James Forman, a civil rights activist, issued what he called a "Black Manifesto to the White Christian Churches and the Jewish Synagogues in the United States of American and All Other Racist Institutions," demanding payment of $500 million in reparations to African Americans. His campaign was not successful. But it was this event that prompted Professor Boris Bittker to subject the issue of black reparations to a sympathetic but lawyer-like analysis. The result was his 1973 classic work, *The Case for Black Reparations,* which Beacon Press has wisely seen fit to bring back into print. Over the intervening thirty years, his book has had a profound impact on both popular and scholarly writings on a wide range of subjects having to do with racial discrimination and remediation, not just with reparations.

Despite the achievements of the Civil Rights Movement of the 1950s and 1960s, he contended then that "the legacy of the

Jim Crow system is still with us" and that meaningful remedies should be provided for the damage done to generations of
African Americans. Where the system of racially segregated
public education was concerned, in particular, it was his view
that the claim for reparations might have the greatest legal
plausibility. Of course circumstances have changed dramati-
cally since 1973 with respect to the concept of reparations both
here and abroad. One consequence of this change has been the
recent filing of reparations lawsuits against several major
corporations and the promise of additional suits against the
federal government and prominent northern private universities. The suits already brought against corporations on behalf
of all African American descendants of slaves seek compensation from the defendants for profits allegedly earned through
their use of slave labor and involvement in the slave trade. The
federal government has been mentioned as a defendant in future reparations litigation on the theory that public officials
guaranteed the viability of slavery and its legacy of racial segregation and discrimination. The universities have been iden-
tified as allegedly benefiting from grants and endowments
traceable to slavery.

At home, as Professor Bittker notes in his postscript in the
form of a preface, which follows, there is the granting by the
federal government of an apology and monetary compensation
to Japanese-Americans subjected to internment during World
War II. There have also been efforts at the state level to compensate African Americans for their victimization in the post–
World War I period at the hands of racist whites. Florida did
so in 1994 by allocating $2 million to nine black survivors of
the 1923 race riot in Rosewood. And the Oklahoma Commission to Study the Tulsa Race Riot of 1921 recommended that
survivors and their descendants be paid reparations for that
uprising in which thousands of whites stormed a prosperous

African American neighborhood, killing at least forty people and destroying homes and businesses.

Internationally, the media reported extensively on the intense wrangling at the United Nations Conference on Racism in Durban, South Africa, in September 2002. The final declaration of that conference acknowledged profound regret over slavery, calling it a "crime against humanity," but declined to embrace reparations as a remedy, or to demand an official apology from those countries involved in the slave trade. There are also the negotiated settlements in which Holocaust victims stand to receive $8 billion in reparations from the governments of Germany, France, and Austria and from Swiss banks. And, finally, the experiences of South Africa's Truth and Reconciliation Commission have had an impact on many African Americans who believe that at least an apology is long overdue here. In that regard, a Gallup Poll in 1997 found that African Americans were in favor of a governmental apology by a two-to-one margin. The coalition of civil rights and civil liberties organizations favoring reparations also appears to be growing.

The current reparations movement and the research and inquiry that it has generated have begun to move our society toward discovering more about the true stories of slavery previously unknown to the general public and familiar to only a handful of historians, at best. It strikes me that the nation is, in a sense, very much like where it was with respect to state-imposed racial segregation in the late 1960s and early 1970s, namely, believing that this form of discrimination was just a "Southern" problem. What we learned was that it was a national one, as, for example, court decision after court decision documented how school boards in the North and West manipulated attendance boundaries to create and maintain racially-segregated public schools. Thus, recent research has established that a northern newspaper, the *Hartford Courant,* published advertisements in support of the sale and capture of slaves. And one of the nation's largest insurance companies, Aetna, learned that it had once insured slave owners against the death of their human chattel. Both the *Hartford Courant* and Aetna offered apologies, once presented with this evidence. In response to the findings with respect to the role that insurance companies may have played with respect to slavery, the State of California enacted a law in 2002 that requires all such companies doing business there to disclose any policies ever issued on the lives of slaves. As a result of their seeking to comply with this new requirement, J. P. Morgan/Chase uncovered evidence of slave policies issued by its predecessor corporations and New York Life appointed an independent task force to investigate its history in this regard. At the very least, all of these developments may serve to clear the air and put aright the record about America's "peculiar institution," chattel slavery.

The reissuance of *The Case for Black Reparations* could not be more timely, consequently. For it provides a valuable analytical framework for any serious consideration of contemporaneous issues of reparations and discrimination. Although circumstances have changed over the past thirty years, the vexing questions about whether and how to remedy old wrongs are still with us.

Preface to the Revised Edition

In the first edition of this book, published in 1973, I labeled the national issue of black reparations a "second American dilemma," echoing the title of Gunnar Myrdal's famous 1944 book, *An American Dilemma,* which massively documented his conclusion that "the Negro problem in America represents a moral lag in the development of the nation." I observed that the dilemma "will seem nonexistent" to those "who reject the idea of reparations because the injury resulting from segregation is too difficult to assess, too great to be susceptible to compensation, or too similar to other wrongs that go uncompensated in an imperfect world." I then ended my examination of the subject, saying:

> We are, or ought to be, at the beginning of a national debate on these questions. I have sought to open the discussion, not to close it.

Although proposals for black reparations have appeared on the country's radar screen from time to time since the publication of this book, they have never been high on the list of issues for public examination, but that status may be in the process of change. In analyzing the subject in 1973, I concentrated on the appalling effects of segregation in our public schools, arguing that a remedy might be found in litigation seeking damages for the then living Afro-Americans who had been compelled by state law to attend segregated schools. This approach, it seemed to me, had the advantage of focusing attention on the identifiable damages to identifiable individuals of a practice that was ruled unconstitutional by the Supreme Court in *Brown v. Board of Education*, decided in 1954. By contrast, I thought that an attempt to obtain reparations from the courts for the effects of slavery, though obviously monstrous, would encounter greater, probably insuperable, barriers, largely because its evils were more attenuated. My 1973 call for a massive class action in the courts, however, did not achieve its objective; and with the passage of thirty years since my book was published, a lawsuit today seeking redress for the damages inflicted by school segregation would very likely be barred by the passage of time, bringing into play various statutes of limitations.

Congress, however, is not subject to a statute of limitations. It can, if it chooses, address wrongs of any type, no matter how attenuated by the passage of time. Thus, recognizing that it is never too late to seek a remedy for a national evil, a bill now before Congress (H.R. 40, 107th Congress, 1st session) proposes:

> To acknowledge the fundamental injustice, cruelty, brutality, and inhumanity of slavery in the United States and the 13 American colonies between 1619 and 1865 and to establish a commission to examine the institution of slavery, subsequently de jure and de facto racial and economic discrimination against African-Americans, and the impact of these forces on living African-Americans, to make recommendations to the Congress on appropriate remedies, and for other purposes.

When I wrote *The Case for Black Reparations,* there were no American guideposts for the remedial commission of the kind proposed by H.R. 40, but an agency of this type was created in 1980 to recommend a mode of redressing the damages to the Japanese-Americans who were relocated and incarcerated during World War II on baseless, flimsy and even trumped-up "evidence." Named the Commission on Wartime Relocation and Interment of Civilians, this organization reported in 1983 that the wartime detention of citizen and resident aliens of Japanese ancestry reflected "race prejudice, war hysteria, and a failure of political leadership," resulting in grave injustices without any individual review or probative evidence; and it recommended the passage of a congressional joint resolution, signed by the president, apologizing for the injustices; the creation of a public education fund foundation to sponsor research and public education; and payment of compensation of $20,000 each to the survivors. These remedial recommendations were subsequently put into effect, though not without delays and scattered legislative and public opposition.

There is an irony in suggesting that this program to redress the damages to relocated and incarcerated Japanese-Americans might supply a guidepost for a program of black reparations, rather than the other way around, given the fact that school segregation was held unconstitutional by a unanimous Supreme Court in *Brown v. Board of Education* (1954), while the Japanese-American exclusion order was upheld by the Supreme Court in 1944 (though by a divided court whose dissenting Justices are today honored for their independence). Still, as Justice Frankfurter once observed, "Wisdom too often never comes, and so one ought not to reject it merely because it comes late."

I am pleased to have my book back in print, thanks to Beacon Press, and I hope that my thoughts will make a contribution to the resolution of this vexing problem.

The Case for Black Reparations

1.

The Black Manifesto

At the first meeting of a Yale Law School seminar on "The Role of the Black Lawyer," a black student put this question to me: "Would the courts award damages to my people for the value of their labor during the days of slavery?" I took his question at face value, and answered "No." I knew that proposals to end slavery often included compensation to the slave owner for his lost "property," but that in the case of the slaves the main economic objective was to keep them from becoming public charges in the future, rather than to pay them for work done in the past. I also knew that the post-emancipation call for "forty acres and a mule" was not answered,[1] so that "the bondsman's two hundred and fifty years of unrequited toil," to use Lincoln's phrase, remained unrequited. Against this background, there seemed to me no likelihood that today's courts would

3

hold that a right to compensation had been inherited by the descendants of the emancipated slaves.

My answer, however, probably mistook the form of the question for its substance. The student's intent was probably to imply that our system of law is shaped by political and economic power and that it serves those who possess that power, not those who live their lives outside the mainstream of American society. Moreover, in putting this proposition to me, he was probably not interested in an exchange of views in order to refine or modify his own conclusions. More likely, he wanted to decide whether I was an unrealistic believer in legal neutrality or a clear-eyed observer of legal bias.

Whatever his purpose and however many levels there were to his question, however, its face value—is or should there be a right to recover for slavery or for the century of segregation that was its aftermath?—seemed weighty to me.

Shortly after this question was posed in my seminar, James Forman interrupted the Sunday morning service at Riverside Church in New York City. Addressing himself "to the White Christian Churches and the Jewish Synagogues in the United States of America and All Other Racist Institutions," he read a Black Manifesto which demanded that the churches and synagogues pay $500 million as "a beginning of the reparations due us as people who have been exploited and degraded, brutalized, killed and persecuted." The amount demanded by the Manifesto, which was adopted by the National Black Economic Development Conference before Forman's action was taken, was to be used to establish a Southern land bank, publishing and printing industries, four audio-visual networks, a research skills center, a training center for teaching skills in community organization and communications, a black labor strike and defense fund, a black university, and several other institutions. To achieve its objectives, the Manifesto called "for the total disruption of selected church-sponsored agencies" by the seizure of their offices, to be held "in trusteeship until our demands are met." It went on to assert that churches and synagogues were only the first target, and that similar demands would be addressed to private business and the federal government.[2]

To no one's surprise, there was immediate and widespread condemnation in the white community of the tactics adopted and advocated by Forman and his group, mingled with conciliatory remarks or expressions of sympathy by a few religious leaders. Some churches initiated programs of assistance to black committees and organizations; but although these programs may have broken with the traditions of their sponsors, they moved only ankle-deep into Forman's pounding surf.[3]

What was most notable about the response to the Black Manifesto, however, was the paucity of analysis. Most commentators addressed themselves solely to Forman's tactics; few had anything to say about reparations as a concept of social justice. To be sure, some white churchmen approached the issue from a moral or theological point of view, but they had little to contribute beyond admissions of guilt and endorsements of repentance. Clergymen who probably regarded self-flagellation as a superstitious remnant of medievalism when practiced in Spain seemed to think it would be a cleansing experience in Scarsdale and Evanston. The secular commentators had even less to say about the substance and underlying premises of the concept of reparations. When the issue was confronted at all, the reaction was consistent with a *New York Times* editorial observation that "there is neither wealth nor wisdom enough in the world to compensate in money for all the wrongs in history."[4] This blinding insight is the conservative counterpart of the revolutionary maxim that you can't make an omelet without breaking eggs.

Failure to come to grips with the idea of reparations has a solid foundation in precedent. For more than a century before Forman came to public attention, spokesmen for very divergent strains of American Negro opinion had put forth a variety of proposals for reparations in the form of cash and land.[5] So far as I know, none of these proposals elicited a favorable response from the white community or even a sober discussion of reparations as a concept. Evidence of this silence is supplied by Gunnar Myrdal's monumental *An American Dilemma* (1944): the forty-page index to this comprehensive work of fourteen hundred pages contains about twenty-five hundred subject entries, but the words "reparations," "compensation," "restitution," and "indemnity" are not among them. This omission has a counterpart in Myrdal's otherwise persuasive theory that the 1865–70 failure to provide the emancipated slaves with an agrarian economic base started us down the fateful road to a segregated society. In his view, a rational economic reform of the South's plantation economy would have included reimbursing slave owners for the loss of their slaves, and seizing but paying for large plantations, with the land divided into small parcels for sale on a long-term installment plan to farmers; but he did not mention the possibility of compensating the emancipated slaves for their years of servitude.[6]

A dedicated German proponent of reparations to Jews persecuted by the Nazi regime has pointed out that this subject has been ignored in German legal and philosophic circles, even though the program of reparations to Jews and other persecuted minorities that was eventually enacted in West Germany has generated a plethora of moral problems and judicial decisions.[7] By turning their backs on this body of law, he has observed, German academicians thrust it into a ghetto, where it was denied the analytic attention that is lavished on every other element of the corpus juris. My aim in this book is to bring the concept of black reparations out of its ghetto. Since it was presented on at least one level as a theory of legal responsibility or liability, I want to see if a lawyer, using the tools of his trade, can clarify its implications. Because my inquiry has spawned more questions than answers, however, this book is an inquest, or perhaps the prelude to an inquest—not a trial. My aim is to stimulate, at last, the debate that was so strikingly missing in the months immediately after Forman's interruption of the Riverside Church service in May 1969.

2.

The Case for Compensation

In his demand for $500 million as black reparations, Forman said:

Fifteen dollars for every black brother and sister in the United States is only a beginning of the reparations due us as people who have been exploited and degraded, brutalized, killed and persecuted.

Although the Black Manifesto does not emphasize and barely even mentions slavery, it is often assumed that the primary objective of reparations is compensation for the value of slave labor. For example, the student's question that inaugurated this inquiry was: "Would the courts award damages to my people for the value of their labor during the days of slavery?" Similarly, in proposing a "Bill of Rights for the Disadvantaged," Martin Luther King, Jr., argued that "[t]he moral justification for special measures for Negroes is rooted in the robberies inherent in the institution of slavery."[8] *The New York Times'* comment on Forman's demands—"There is neither wealth nor wisdom enough in the world to compensate in money for all the wrongs in history"—similarly implies that proposals for reparations focus on the injustices of the distant past. This idea has also been fed by several academic studies by economic historians of the value of slave labor. Indeed, the most recent of these explicitly relates its findings to the amount of compensation demanded by several black groups; it estimates the present-day value of "unpaid black equity in the slave industry" at between $448 and $995 billion, and praises the "accounting ability" of one black group (the Republic of New Africa) because the dollar level of its demands coincides almost precisely with the author's own estimates.[9]

This preoccupation with slavery, in my opinion, has stultified the discussion of black reparations by implying that the only issue is the correction of an ancient injustice, thus inviting the reply that the wrongs were committed by persons long since dead, whose profits may well have been dissipated during their own lifetimes or their descendants' and whose moral responsibility should not be visited upon succeeding generations, let alone upon wholly unrelated persons. In his subtle and perceptive *Who Speaks for the Negro?* Robert Penn Warren says of the idea that society owes "back wages" for slavery:

> The whole notion of untangling the "debts" of history smacks of fantasy. Would the descendants of an Athenian helot of the fifth century B.C., assuming that such a relationship could be established, have a claim today on the Greek government? And with or without accrued interest? Would the descendant of a mill girl in Lowell, Massachusetts, who died of lint-lungs in

1845, have a claim on Washington, D.C., in 1965? Or would it be Boston? . . .

And while we are on the subject, let us branch out and try to calculate how many explosion-prone trade guns, ankers of rum, and iron bars the Nigerian government owes what percentage of the twenty million American Negroes—those things being the common currency the ancestors of the said Nigerians demanded in payment for the ancestors of the said American Negroes whom the ancestors of the Nigerians had bagged in the bush and put up for sale. The whole thing is a grisly farce. Come to think of it, it smacks not of fantasy, but of Bedlam.[10]

When black reparations are viewed solely as belated payment for the value of slave labor, this type of response is not easily rebutted. But slavery was only a necessary, not a sufficient, condition for today's compensatory proposals. If the emancipation of blacks during and after the Civil War had been followed by their absorption into the mainstream of American life, it is conceivable that the only identifiable residue of slavery in today's world would be cultural—the folklore, songs, literature, and myths of an earlier era. A hundred years ago, there were many observers who predicted this outcome, vividly expressed in the comments of T. Thomas Fortune, an ex-slave, the leading black journalist of his day, a founder of the Afro-American League, and later an editor of Marcus Garvey's *Negro World:*

I am not seriously concerned about the future political status of the black man of the South. He has talent; he has ambition; he possesses a rare fund of eloquence, of wit and humor, and these will carry him into the executive chambers of States, the halls of legislation and on to the bench of the judiciary. You can't bar him out; you can't repress him: he will make his way. God has planted in his very nature those elements which constitute the stock-in-trade of the American politician—ready elo-

.quence, rich humor, quick perception—and you may rest assured he will use all of them to the very best advantage.

I know of municipalities in the South to-day [1884], where capable colored men are regularly voted into responsible positions by the best white men of their cities. And why not? Do not colored men vote white men into office? And, pray, is the white man less magnanimous than the black man? Perish the thought! No; the politics of the South will readily adjust themselves to the best interest of the people; be very sure of this. And the future rulers of the South will not all be white, nor will they all be black: they will be a happy commingling of the two peoples.

And thus with the so-called "war of races:" it will pass away and leave not a trace behind. It is based upon condition and color prejudice—two things which cannot perpetuate themselves. . . .

Already I have seen in the South the black and the white farm laborer, working side by side for a black landlord; already I have seen in the South a black and a white brick-mason (and carpenters as well) working upon a building side by side, under a colored contractor. And we are not yet two decades from the surrender of Robert E. Lee and the manumission of the black slave.

I have no disposition to infuriate any white man of the South, by placing a red flag before him; we simply desire to accustom him to look upon a picture which his grand-children will not, because of the frequency of the occurrence, regard with anything more heart-rending than complacent indifference.[11]

If this vision of an integrated and equal society had become a reality, the student's question that began my inquiry into reparations—"Would the courts award damages to my people for the value of their labor during the days of slavery?"—would be less disquieting. The answer might be: "No, but slavery was outlawed a long time ago; a century of equality has intervened; you lead the same life as the descendants of a slaveholding planter; however strong the claim for compensation was in 1865, it is by now too stale to arouse my sense of injustice." There is merit in the argument that the Americans of today, who would have to pay the bill, are no more responsible for ante-bellum slavery in the South than for serfdom in pre-1861 Czarist Russia.

But to concentrate on slavery is to understate the case for compensation, so much so that one might almost suspect that the distant past is serving to suppress the ugly facts of the recent past and of contemporary life. In actuality, slavery was followed not by a century of equality but by a mere decade of faltering progress, repeatedly checked by violence. The hope kindled in the era of Reconstruction was snuffed out by the political settlement of 1877, and the Negro's "proper place" was soon defined as a status of inferiority, described succinctly by C. Vann Woodward:

> In the early years of the twentieth century, it was becoming clear that the Negro would be effectively disfranchised throughout the South, that he would be firmly relegated to the lower rungs of the economic ladder, and that neither equality nor aspirations for equality in any department of life were for him.
>
> The public symbols and constant reminders of his inferior position were the segregation statutes, or "Jim Crow" laws. They constituted the most elaborate and formal expression of sovereign white opinion upon the subject. In bulk and detail as well as in effectiveness of enforcement the segregation codes were comparable with the black codes of the old regime, though the laxity that mitigated the harshness of the black codes was replaced by a rigidity that was more typical of the segregation code. That code lent the sanction of law to a racial ostracism that extended to churches and schools, to housing and jobs, to eating and drinking. Whether by law or by custom, that ostracism eventually extended to virtually all forms of public trans-

portation, to sports and recreations, to hospitals, orphanages, prisons, and asylums, and ultimately to funeral homes, morgues, and cemeteries.[12]

As a legal system, segregation received its constitutional imprimatur in 1896, when the Supreme Court held in *Plessy v. Ferguson* that states could require the separation of blacks from whites in railroad cars. Segregation was consistent with the equal-protection clause of the Fourteenth Amendment (providing that no state shall "deny to any person within its jurisdiction the equal protection of the laws"), according to the Court, because:

> The object of the [Fourteenth] amendment was undoubtedly to enforce the absolute equality of the two races before the law, but in the nature of things it could not have been intended to abolish distinctions based upon color, or to enforce social, as distinguished from political, equality, or a commingling of the two races upon terms unsatisfactory to either. Laws permitting, and even requiring, their separation in places where they are liable to be brought into contact do not necessarily imply the inferiority of either race to the other. . . .

Responding to the argument that the "separate but equal" doctrine might be employed to sanction the gratuitous humiliation of Negroes (e.g., "requiring colored people to walk upon one side of the street, and white people upon the other, or requiring white men's houses to be painted white, and colored men's black"), the Court said:

> The reply to all this is that every exercise of the police power must be reasonable, and extend only to such laws as are enacted in good faith for the promotion of the public good, and not for the annoyance or oppression of a particular class.[13]

Reading these words today, one is staggered by their lack of realism. Is it possible that the Justices who wrote the opinion in *Plessy v. Ferguson* did not realize that in practice the physical facilities for blacks were, and would be, systematically inferior in physical conditions, let alone in social and psychological consequences? They were not, after all, college professors who had never met a payroll, but men of affairs. The cynic may assert that they intended to endorse in advance the inequalities that in fact prevailed; indeed, the sole dissenting justice, John Marshall Harlan, came close to making this point by his assertion that an official badge of inferiority, "as all will admit, is the real meaning" of the legislation upheld in *Plessy* and that "the thin disguise" of equality "will not mislead anyone."[14] A bitter irony of *Plessy v. Ferguson* is that the plaintiff asserted that his "one-eighth African blood" was "not discernible" (though it made him a Negro under Louisiana law) and that the Jim Crow statute deprived him of "the reputation of being white" and excluded him "from the friendship and companionship of the white man."[15]

So patent was the function of the legislation upheld by the Court in the *Plessy* case that one might suspect "separate but equal" of being a code phrase, understood—and intended to be understood—by public officials everywhere as meaning "separate even though unequal." In common parlance, blacks are said to attend "segregated" schools, not whites; the verbal convention accurately implies that it is blacks rather than whites who are separated from the mainstream of society. Whether or not *Plessy v. Ferguson* was disingenuous in using the term "equal," it ushered in a long period when despite rampant inequalities, public officials, lawyers, judges, and even Negro organizations evidently acknowledged that the second adjective in the phrase "separate but equal" was for practical purposes a dead letter. Not until the nineteen-thirties was there a serious attempt to pour content into the requirement of equality,[16] and by then the disparities were so monumental that their correction would have been almost as unsettling to the South as full enforcement of *Brown v. Board of Education.*

In the meantime, the "separate but equal" doctrine became the legal foundation for state laws requiring segregation in schools, libraries, courthouses, and other public facilities, as well as in such privately owned places of public accommodation as restaurants, hotels, theaters, and buses. Lest it be thought that this network of statutes was a legacy from the days of slavery, it should be noted that many of them were enacted after *Plessy v. Ferguson* and that some are as recent as the nineteen-twenties and thirties.[17]

Parallel to these state and local laws requiring segregated facilities but lacking their support in the "separate but equal" doctrine, there developed a host of other discriminatory practices by public officials. Full citizenship was in effect denied by the discriminatory enforcement of state laws governing the right to vote, to serve on juries, and to run for public office. Although the courts intervened sporadically to correct violations, these occasional victories were at best symbolic, leaving the basic pattern intact. And there was rarely even the consolation of a symbol in many areas where discrimination was practiced but was less easily proved, viz., in the panoply of routine state and municipal functions, ranging from police protection to the paving of streets, from civil service jobs to the sentences imposed for violations of laws, from the granting of licenses to courtesy by public officials, from the message conveyed in schoolbooks to the implicit assumptions of school guidance counselors. The understandable emphasis of civil rights groups on school buildings, housing, voting, employment, and police practices has obscured these more mundane but similarly unjustified inequalities in public services. In a decision that may presage a burst of judicial activity in this area, however, a federal court recently found that the Negro neighborhood of one small town in Mississippi suffered from systematic deficiencies in such municipal services as the paving and lighting of streets, sanitary and storm sewers, fire hydrants, and traffic-control signs, and ordered corrective measures to be taken by the municipality.[18] I know of no general survey of this area, but it hardly takes blind faith to believe that similar deficiencies are endemic to black neighborhoods throughout the country. Lacking any pretense to constitutional validity but simultaneously resistant to judicial correction, these forms of official discrimination were common in the North as well as the South; the Negro's "place" could be defined by unequal enforcement of the law, even in the absence of a formal system of legal segregation.

Though the litany of discrimination by public agencies is all too familiar, a word about the complicity of the federal government is in order, since federal funding would be essential to any program of reparations on a scale matching the injury to be redressed. Perhaps no more need be said than that an officially segregated school system was maintained under Congressional authority in the nation's capitol until 1954 and that legal provisions for segregated schools, though unenforceable under *Brown v. Board of Education,* appear in the District of Columbia Code even today.[19] As late as the eve of World War II, there were segregated lunchrooms and other facilities in many federal buildings, and segregation in the armed forces, with minor exceptions, was the order of the day until well after the war.[20] Less dramatic and rigid, but perhaps even more important because so pervasive, were the discriminatory policies of federal agencies administering residential and business loans and guarantees, public housing projects, agricultural extension services, farm-price supports, and other economic and social programs that have only gradually been subjected to the constitutional standard of equality that in .theory has always been applicable. When practiced by the federal government, segregation and discrimination were defended less often as independently justifiable than as an unavoidable accommodation to Southern white attitudes, especially in the case of the armed forces and federal offices in the South. Even if this knee-jerk explanation is accepted, it does not diminish the federal contribution to the depressed economic and social status of blacks, especially since federal discrimination was a model that simultaneously reinforced Southern intransigence and invited Northern imitation.

Thus, as slavery receded into the background, it was succeeded by a caste system embodying white supremacy. The clash between the Negro's clearly defined place and the American ideal of equality was the American Dilemma described by Myrdal. It created a tension in the minds of many whites, but as he so clearly saw, a central part of the dilemma was the lack of public challenge to white supremacy or to the propriety of segregation. The ice began to crack in the nineteen-thirties, when Hitler's racial laws invited comparison with our domestic rules and thus stimulated soul-searching; but segregation as a system remained virtually intact until the increased social, economic, and geographical mobility that accompanied World War II created practical difficulties in the preservation of the old folkways. These trends, which accelerated after the war, paved the way for the overruling of *Plessy v. Ferguson* by the Supreme Court's 1954 decision in *Brown v. Board of Education.*

Although the *Brown* case was concerned with segregation in the public school system, it was only in other public and quasi-public facilities—libraries, parks, theaters, hotels, railroad stations, buses, etc.—that the ouster of Jim Crow practices was prompt and substantially complete. (Occasional suggestions that "nothing has changed" are stimulated by understandable despair at the sluggishness of reform, but they are also belied by the facts. A proposal to reinstate legally separated waiting rooms, drinking fountains, and dining facilities would not be shrugged off as a mere continuation of existing practices, but would instead be properly denounced as a revolutionary attempt to turn back the clock.) As to the desegregation of public schools, the Supreme Court's initial order was to proceed "with all deliberate speed," a formulation that in practice functioned more like a maximum than a minimum speed limit. Fourteen years later (1968), the Supreme Court found that "very little progress had been made in many areas where dual school systems had historically been maintained by operation of state laws," and in 1969 the Court announced that the "all deliberate speed" standard was no longer "constitutionally permissible," and that "the obligation of every school district is to terminate dual school systems at once." Repeating this injunction in 1971, the Court also commented that "[n]othing in our national experience prior to 1955 prepared anyone for dealing with changes and adjustments of the magnitude and complexity encountered since then."[21]

In a postscript to the twentieth-anniversary edition of *An American Dilemma*, Mr. Myrdal's collaborator said that the change in race relations during the period 1942–62 "appeared as one of the most rapid in the history of human relations." Because a judgment of this kind cannot be divorced from the commentator's perspective, Frederick Douglass' less conclusive but more explicitly contextual epitome of President Lincoln's position on slavery seems preferable:

> Viewed from the genuine abolition ground, Mr. Lincoln seemed tardy, cold, dull, and indifferent; but measuring him by the sentiment of his country, a sentiment he was bound as a statesman to consult, he was swift, zealous, radical, and determined.[22]

Whether the changes since the end of World War II and the *Brown* decision are viewed as glacier-slow or unexpectedly rapid, however, one thing is clear: the legacy of the Jim Crow system is still with us. The status of American blacks today stems unmistakably from the years when segregation enjoyed the nihil obstat of *Plessy v. Ferguson,* and no one who is sensitive to the persistent effects of deep-seated social customs, especially when reinforced or stimulated by the legal system, can doubt that the life of blacks in America will bear for decades the scars of a century of discrimination. Even if the doctrine of *Brown v. Board of Education* had been enforced with the vigor that its most zealous champions demanded, it is unlikely that black youths—let alone older people—would enjoy full equality in today's America. But we need not speculate: the enforcement process was in fact slow and halting.

Against this background, the first point to be made about proposals for black reparations is that they seek to redress injuries caused by a system of legally imposed segregation that was eventually held in *Brown v. Board of Education* to violate the equal-protection clause of the Fourteenth Amendment. I do not mean to imply that there is a constitutional right to be compensated for governmental misconduct, or that it has been customary for the courts to create such a remedy on their own initiative. To the contrary. The only provision in the Constitution for pecuniary redress is the Fifth Amendment's prohibition against the taking of private property for public use without just compensation; other violations of a citizen's rights are usually redressed solely by nonpecuniary remedies unless Congress has expressly provided that damages are to be paid. Thus, the remedy for malapportionment is a judicially supervised reapportionment; the remedy for the improper selection of a jury or the wrongful admission of evidence at a trial is a new trial for the losing party; the remedy for an erroneous denial of a license is an order requiring it to be granted; and so on. These instances of governmental misconduct may cause emotional or pecuniary damage to the citizen, yet the normal approach of the courts is to eliminate the condition for the future rather than to provide pecuniary solace for the past. This principle is not without its exceptions, however, and a recent Supreme Court decision may pave the way to its relaxation.

In *Bivens v. Six Unknown Agents of the Federal Bureau of Narcotics,* the petitioner alleged that agents of the Federal Bureau of Narcotics entered his apartment, and

> manacled [him] in front of his wife and children, . . . threatened to arrest the entire family . . . searched the apartment from stem to stern . . . [and took him] to the federal courthouse in Brooklyn, where he was interrogated, booked, and subjected to a visual strip search.

Asserting that the agents had no search warrant, lacked probable cause for arresting him, and used unreasonable force—all in violation of the Fourth Amendment, prohibiting "unreasonable searches and seizures"—the petitioner sued to recover damages for his "humiliation, embarrassment, and mental suffering." Although Congress has not enacted a statute explicitly providing for the payment of damages when federal officials violate the Fourth Amendment, a majority of the Supreme Court held that such a remedy was inherent in the Constitution.[23] Three justices dissented, not because they objected on principle to compensating injured citizens for governmental misconduct, but because they held to the narrower theory that Congress rather than the courts should take the initiative in framing such a remedy.

Congress and the state legislatures have in fact enacted a host of laws awarding damages for governmental misconduct ranging from the negligence of government employees in driving postal trucks to the erroneous conviction and incarceration of innocent persons.[24] One of these laws, which imposes liability on state and local officials who subject anyone to the deprivation of his federal Constitutional or statutory rights, was cited by Justice Hugo Black (dissenting in the *Bivens* case) as a model that might be broadened by Congress to cover misconduct by federal officials. (It will be discussed further in the next chapter.) One might well wish Congress and the state legislatures to act more boldly to compensate the citizen whose rights were infringed by official misconduct, or to enact a general plan of compensation in place of these sporadic instances of legislative compassion. The case for black reparations, however, need not rest on the theory that damages should be paid for every species of improper official conduct. We are in the realm of legislative discretion. More than any other form of official misconduct, racial discrimination against blacks was systematic, unrelenting, authorized at the highest governmental levels, and practiced by large segments of the population. These facts argue for a legislative plan of reparations in this area, even if other instances of unconstitutional official action are left to be redressed solely by nonmonetary remedies.[25]

Is the case for compensation weakened by the fact that segregation was sanctioned by the "separate but equal" doctrine from 1896, when it was enunciated by *Plessy v. Ferguson*, until 1954, when *Plessy* was overruled by *Brown v. Board of Education?* I think not. We need not employ the fiction that this doctrine was itself unconstitutional during its hegemony in order to free ourselves of its influence. "Wisdom too often never comes, and so one ought not to reject it merely because it comes late."[26] If, even though only by hindsight, conduct is seen to be both unconstitutional and abhorrent, the fact that it was thought permissible, neutral, or benign when committed may be a mitigating element in assessing blame or guilt, but it is surely not a reason to refrain from making amends. When Congress acted in 1946 to redress some of the wrongs committed while America was pursuing her manifest destiny by pushing back the Indians, it created an Indian Claims Commission to adjudicate a wide range of claims by Indian tribes. These included not merely claims under treaties that had been violated by the United States but also "claims which would result if the treaties, contracts, and agreements between the [Indian tribal] claimant and the United States were revised on the ground of fraud, duress, unconscionable consideration, mutual or unilateral mistake, whether of law or fact, or any other ground cognizable by a court of equity" and "claims based upon fair and honorable dealings that are not recognized by any existing rule of law or equity." This ideal of "fair and honorable dealings" is a more amorphous standard than courts are ordinarily handed by Congress, and they have only just begun to give it tangible form,[27] but as abstractions go, it would be a suitable one for Congress to keep in mind in passing on the reasonableness of the demand for black reparations.

Moreover, when an old legal doctrine is overturned in favor of a new one, the usual principle is to "apply the law as it is at the time, not as it once was."[28] This principle has been the subject of stormy judicial debate and intense scholarly scrutiny in recent years, primarily because of the numerous new rules of criminal procedure (relating to such matters as pre-interrogation warnings, the use of confessions, and the right to counsel) that have been promulgated by the Supreme Court in recent years. When the procedural rights of a defendant are enlarged in a particular case, the new rule is ordinarily applied to all other defendants who are awaiting trial or whose cases are on appeal, even though the alleged crime was committed when the superseded rule was in effect. The status of convictions obtained under the old rule is more troublesome, however, if the defendant has already exhausted all of his normal appellate rights. If his case is reopened, and a conviction of many years' standing is reversed under the new rule, a retrial may well be impossible because memories have faded or witnesses have died or disappeared. Recognizing this, the courts have sometimes held that "old" cases are not entitled to the benefit of a new procedural rule, unless Congress chooses as a matter of discretion to authorize its retrospective application.[29] Whatever may be the merits of this approach (which has been regularly criticized by dissenting judges and commentators), it in no way undercuts the case for a legislatively enacted program of black reparations. The fact that segregation by law was regarded as constitutional from 1896 to 1954 is not inconsistent with a Congressional decision to provide compensation for the damages it inflicted on its victims.

Black reparations, then, would serve to redress injuries suffered under a legal system that was held by *Brown v. Board of Education* to violate the Constitution. Moreover, even before the *Brown* case was decided, segregation as actually practiced consistently and deliberately violated the "separate but equal" doctrine of *Plessy v. Ferguson*. Closely related to the pervasive inferiority of segregated facilities for blacks, but geographically more widespread, was the unequal enforcement of the law. As pointed out earlier, inequalities in the administration of such public functions and services as police protection, government employment, and voter registration were nakedly improper and could not be cloaked by the "separate but equal" doctrine. There are many shortcomings in our treatment of the losers in our society, but none matches this record of institutionalized deprivation of a group's constitutional rights. In this respect, the case for black reparations is even stronger than the case for compensating the victims of poverty or miscarriages of criminal justice.

Finally, there is the fallout of official action upon the economic, political, and social life of the country. Segregation was compulsory not only in publicly owned facilities in the South but also in privately owned restaurants, hotels, and theaters. No room was left for private choice—for freedom of association—in these areas. An ironic aspect of the concept of freedom of association was that the state and federal courts enforced restrictive covenants in the transfer of property until forbidden to do so by the Supreme Court in 1948.[30] Until then, if a group of neighbors agreed not to sell or rent their residences to blacks, their agreement could be enforced by court order, despite a change of mind on the part of any individual owner, unless all of his neighbors released him from the restrictive covenant. The result of all this was that big business, labor unions, fraternal societies, social clubs, charitable organizations, churches, political parties, banks, land developers, and all the other institutions of local, regional, and national life felt the influence of official discriminatory action, even if they were not subject to formal regulations. The pervasive impact of official policy on private life is also illustrated by the anti-miscegenation laws, imposing legal restrictions on marriage itself. In subordinating the personal wishes of the parties these laws resembled the legal prohibitions against incestuous marriages and marriages by persons suffering from venereal disease; and it is fair to say that the violation of any of these three taboos stimulated a similar sense of public outrage.

It is impossible to know what our society would be like today if unalloyed personal preference had been allowed full sway after slavery was abolished. Without official segregation, would we have become an integrated nation? Or would "personal" prejudice have produced segregation, first in the home, then in Mrs. Murphy's boardinghouse, and then in business and politics? For those who accept William Graham Sumner's dictum that "law-ways cannot alter folkways," law is an effect of social custom, not a cause. Some may believe that we are born with prejudice or that the dynamics of family life inexorably inculcate suspicion or hostility toward strangers, at least those of a different color, and that segregation as a legal system merely regularized or even mitigated these tendencies. Possibly, however, the exotic stranger is innately appealing rather than repellent to those whose views are not coerced by law. Unfortunately, we have no science of social evolution capable of producing a model of the United States as it would have been if blacks had come here as voluntary immigrants rather than as slaves, or if emancipation had been followed by the integrated society envisioned by T. Thomas Fortune in the passage quoted earlier in this chapter.[31]

As a working hypothesis to fill this vacuum, I am prepared

to accept the theory that statutes, ordinances, and other official actions have been the predominant source of the racial discrimination that has blighted our public and private life. If accepted, this premise is a justification for publicly financed reparations to the victims of discrimination, even though some of the damage may stem from "private" behavior that might have occurred in the absence of official encouragement or even in violation of official prohibitions.

In basing the case for black reparations so firmly on a century of official conduct that in time was held to violate the Fourteenth Amendment (and, in the case of the federal government, the due-process clause of the Fifth Amendment), I do not mean to suggest that moral philosophy is irrelevant to the issue. For one thing, reliance on the Fourteenth Amendment implies acceptance of its ethical underpinnings. And since the Fourteenth Amendment requires not the payment of compensation for official misconduct but only its cessation, it is not enough of a foundation by itself. The advocate of reparations must also contend that justice requires compensating past injuries rather than merely forbidding their repetition. In making this plea for legislative action, however, he can persuasively assert that the Fourteenth Amendment is a national commitment to a standard of conduct, whose scope has been made definite for our day by the decision in *Brown v. Board of Education*, and that the only open question is the proper remedy for its breach. Were it not for the Fourteenth Amendment, the morality of segregation —a larger question but, as it happens, an easier one to answer —would also be at issue in the advocacy of black reparations.

The case for black reparations, of course, cannot be judged in isolation; though vast, our nation's resources are not unlimited, and there are other meritorious claims. A prominent black opponent of reparations, Bayard Rustin, argues that "as a purely racial demand, its effect must be to isolate blacks from the white poor with whom they have common economic interests."[32] This problem of competition among worthy but insatiable claimants for limited resources is discussed in a later chapter. I will confine myself here to a brief comment on a common reaction to the demand for black reparations, epitomized by *The New York Times* when it dismissed James Forman's demands: "There is neither wealth nor wisdom enough in the world to compensate in money for all the wrongs in history." To point out that Forman was asking for the redress of one wrong, not all, is an insufficient response. A better response is the counter-question: Should no wrongs be corrected unless all can be? In both public and private life, we constantly compare competing demands for the redress of injustice, knowing full well that the pit is bottomless, especially since the amelioration of one ill can cause a previously tolerable condition to seem degrading by comparison. This inquiry into black reparations presupposes a society that is prepared to respond to the most meritorious of these claims, rather than dismissing all of them as man's ineluctable fate.

Because "all the wrongs in history" cannot be righted, it is ordinarily wiser to address recent rather than ancient ones. Time is a great physician; if it does not cure an ill, it may at least dissipate its effects. In this spirit, Germany instituted a reparations program after World War II for Jews and other victims of Nazi persecution, even though Egypt was not concurrently paying compensation for what Pharaoh did to the ancient Hebrews. Similarly, the Indian Claims Commission is authorized to rectify violations of our treaties with Indian tribes and to act favorably on claims under the "fair and honorable dealings" standard, even though the tribes presenting the claims may have acquired their territories by conquest from other Indians (before the white man came to America, or between that time and the westward push of the United States) and are not simultaneously offering to redress these wrongs.

In these comments on black reparations, I have focused on the wrongs of the recent past, the consequences of which are everywhere to be seen; slavery has figured only because of its continuing influence on black–white relations after the Civil War. As suggested above, had segregation not been enforced by law, the residue of slavery might be hard to identify today. If this were so, it would be quixotic to try to remedy the injustices of slavery by compensating today's blacks for the value of slave labor extracted from their ancestors more than a century ago, though compensation in 1865 for the blacks' forced labor would certainly have been appropriate.[33]

Time may also mitigate an injustice because the intended victim has made a virtue of necessity. For the Jews in medieval ghettos and in the Russian Pale of Settlement, for example, isolation served as a preservative for their traditions. They enjoyed an intense communal life, free from the values of the world outside; and no scales can balance the Talmud, which they saved, against Voltaire, whom they foreswore. In such a case, compensation for segregation, however viciously motivated, may seem inappropriate when the passage of time has made it impossible to say whether profit or loss predominated. To be sure, there is a similar conflict between centrifugal and centripetal forces among American blacks: "open occupancy" in private housing and low-rent projects in the suburbs may cost the inner city's black-power movement some of its leaders and members; an integrated school may pursue "ethnic" studies with cool impartiality, but an all-black school may give black studies a place of honor; those who are accepted everywhere may be at home nowhere. The day may come when the lingering effects of official segregation will coincide with voluntary self-separation. Talk of black reparations will then be outmoded. Notwithstanding the isolationist trends in black life today, however, racial discrimination has not proved to be a blessing in disguise. Unless and until it is, the case for compensation cannot be regarded as barred by the passage of time.

3.

An Alternative Scenario: Suit under Section 1983 for Damages for Deprivation of Constitutional Rights

When holding (in the opinion discussed in the previous chapter) that Bivens was entitled to compensation for humiliation and embarrassment if the invasion of his apartment by federal narcotics agents constituted an unreasonable search and seizure in violation of the Fourth Amendment, the Supreme Court remarked: "Historically, damages have been regarded as the ordinary remedy for an invasion of personal interests in liberty."[34] This observation suggests the possibility that a system of black reparations, at least in embryo, is secreted in existing law; and this in turn suggests that we explore the subject by imagining an alternative scenario to Forman's reading of the Black Manifesto to the startled worshipers in Riverside Church on May 4, 1969. Let us assume that one of the black students compelled to go to an all-black school in a state whose school segregation law was held unconstitutional in 1954 had consulted a lawyer to

30

find out if he could recover damages for this violation of his constitutional rights. Pointing to the Supreme Court's statement in the *Brown* case that segregated education impairs the "educational and mental development" of black children and "generates a feeling of inferiority as to their status in the community that may affect their hearts and minds in a way unlikely ever to be undone," the student—whom I shall call William Brown—might have asked, "If my school gave me an inferior education, why can't I be paid for my injuries?"

The innocent question might have seemed naïve to the hypothetical lawyer, but if it jolted him out of his complacency and impelled him to search the United States Code, he would have found a statute, Section 1983 of Title 42, which seems to bear on William Brown's problem. It provides that

> Every person who, under color of any statute . . . of any State or Territory, subjects . . . any citizen of the United States . . . to the deprivation of any rights . . . secured by the Constitution and laws, shall be liable to the party injured in an action at law, suit in equity, or other proper proceeding for redress.

Section 1983 was enacted a century ago as Section 1 of the Ku Klux Act, whose principal purpose was to deal with the terrorism perpetrated in the South by the Ku Klux Klan and similar groups in the years immediately following the Civil War. Because the Ku Klux Klan's "invisible government" usurped the functions of the legitimate state authorities, Section 1983 might at first glance seem to be concerned only with similar acts by unauthorized private persons, and to be inapplicable to the maintenance of segregated schools by duly elected state and local officials. In point of fact, however, the courts have repeatedly held that Section 1983 applies to action by a public official that conforms to state law if it simultaneously violates a citizen's federal rights.[35] Conversely, the courts were troubled for many years over whether Section 1983 applied to the seemingly easier case of behavior that violated both state and federal law, such as a policeman's search of a private residence without a proper warrant or a warden's use of excessive force against a prisoner.

The Supreme Court did not lay this issue to rest until 1961, when it decided *Monroe v. Pape,* whose facts resembled *Bivens v. Six Unknown Agents of the Federal Bureau of Narcotics,* except that the alleged misconduct was committed by local rather than federal officers:

> The complaint alleges that 13 Chicago police officers broke into petitioners' home in the early morning, routed them from bed, made them stand naked in the living room, and ransacked every room, emptying drawers and ripping mattress covers. It further alleges that Mr. Monroe was then taken to the police station and detained on "open" charges for 10 hours, while he was interrogated about a two-day-old murder, that he was not taken before a magistrate though one was accessible, that he was not permitted to call his family or attorney, that he was subsequently released without criminal charges being preferred against him. It is alleged that the officers had no search warrant and no arrest warrant. . . .

The defendant policeman argued that if these allegations were true, their conduct violated Illinois law and was therefore not committed "under color" of state law within the meaning of Section 1983. Accepting this theory, the lower courts dismissed the complaint with the observation that the plaintiffs "are not without their remedy in the state court," a roundabout way of saying that they could recover damages under state law and hence did not need the federal remedy of Section 1983. The Supreme Court, however, reversed the lower court, holding that even though the alleged misconduct violated state law, it was nevertheless committed "under color" of state law as that term is used in Section 1983 because the policeman were "clothed with the authority of state law" when they entered the plaintiffs' home, took one of them to the police station, and questioned him about the commission of a crime.[36] The narrower view that officials act "under color" of state law when their conduct *is* authorized by the state was obviously also endorsed, indeed swallowed up, by the broader interpretation thus placed by the Court on Section 1983.

Justice Frankfurter dissented in *Monroe v. Pape,* arguing that Section 1983 was enacted to supply a federal remedy for violations of a citizen's rights by state and local officials only if he could not gain redress in the state courts. In his view, an invasion that violated state law was not committed "under color" of state law unless the state courts refused to grant an appropriate remedy for the official's misconduct. He went on to assert that the majority's interpretation converted Section 1983 into a law to regulate the daily business "of every traffic policeman, every registrar of elections, every city inspector or investigator, every clerk in every municipal licensing bureau in this country" by permitting their behavior to be reviewed by the federal courts whenever a plaintiff alleged an invasion of his federal rights. Fearful that *Monroe v. Pape* might produce such a federal octopus, some commentators have urged the Supreme Court to limit the decision in order to curb its potential for federal intervention in the administration of state law. Conversely, the Frankfurter interpretation of Section 1983 has been criticized by others as an unsympathetically narrow view of a statute intended by Congress to be a sweeping safeguard against misconduct by state and local officials.[37]

For our purposes, these competing assertions are beside

the point. This is because even the narrower view of Section 1983, if applied to school segregation in the manner suggested hereafter, would produce enough legal business to swamp the federal courts even if all other suitors under it were turned away. As Justice Frankfurter put the point:

> . . . Congress . . . legislated to reach a state officer enforcing an unconstitutional law. . . . If a plaintiff can show that defendant is acting pursuant to the specific terms of a state statute or of a municipal ordinance, [Section 1983] will apply.[38]

Armed with the knowledge that Section 1983 applies to public action that both conforms to state law and violates a citizen's federal rights, the lawyer in my scenario files a complaint in a federal district court, alleging that the school-child was deprived of his right to attend a nonsegregated school by the local school board, which was acting not merely "under color" of state law but in strict compliance with it. The complaint goes on to allege that neither abolition of these unconstitutional laws nor speedy desegregation of the local school system will adequately redress the plaintiff's injury, since he has now graduated; and since the school board's violation of the equal-protection clause of the Fourteenth Amendment saddled him with an inferior education, the only proper remedy is a payment of money damages as compensation for his loss. The complaint sticks very close to the phraseology of Section 1983. I have avoided innovation in the language of the complaint not so much to imply that lawyers are timid (though they may be) as to suggest that the concept of reparations is familiar and conservative. In other words, it can wear a three-button suit, as well as a dashiki.

Since the complaint tracks the language of Section 1983 with high fidelity in alleging that the defendants acted under color of state law in maintaining a segregated school system, and that this practice deprived the plaintiff of rights secured to him by the federal Constitution, and since the defendants can hardly controvert these allegations, what more is required by Section 1983 than proof of the plaintiff's damages? But before reaching the startling conclusion that Section 1983 now provides a system of reparations for at least one species of racial discrimination, we must probe further. Is it possible that Congress really intended Section 1983 to impose personal liability on state officers who faithfully complied with state law and were not warned that compliance with their official instructions would violate the federal Constitution? This is the question to which we should now direct our attention.

4.

Liability for the Faithful Performance of Official Duties?

Section 1983 provides that a person who, under color of state law, deprives any citizen of his federal rights "shall be liable to the party injured in an action at law, suit in equity, or other proper proceeding for redress." An "action in law" is ordinarily a lawsuit to compel the defendant to pay damages for an injury committed in the past, as in my hypothetical suit by a pupil compelled to attend a segregated school. A "suit in equity," on the other hand, is usually a lawsuit to compel the defendant to take corrective action in the future, such as the assignment of pupils to schools without regard to race, the transportation of children from one school zone to another, or the promotion of teachers on a nondiscriminatory basis. This kind of "suit in equity," brought under Section 1983, is regularly employed by parents, civil rights groups, and the federal government to combat segregation in schools and other public facilities. Since the courts routinely

36

order local school boards to stop segregating schoolchildren by race, one might well assume that an action for damages caused by segregation in the past would not present any special difficulties. Whether the plaintiff wants to go to an integrated school in the future or to be compensated for being assigned to a segregated school in the past, or both, the crux of the complaint is that segregation, in the words of Section 1983, "subjects [him or her] . . . to the deprivation of rights . . . secured by the Constitution."

Even so, there is a difference between looking forward and looking backward.[39] For almost sixty years before the Supreme Court held in *Brown v. Board of Education* (1954) that it was unconstitutional, segregation in public schools was almost universally assumed to be legally permissible under *Plessy v. Ferguson.* This is quite irrelevant in framing a judicial decree that will govern a school board's future behavior: its belief in the constitutional validity of segregation can hardly be accepted as a reason for continuing the practice. Once condemned, the only extension that can be justified is a transitional period to permit its orderly phasing out. When the members of a school board are asked to pay damages for their behavior during the years when segregation was widely if not unanimously believed to be constitutionally permissible, however, a different issue arises. Even an uncompromising opponent of segregation might doubt the fairness of imposing legal liability on them in these circumstances, contenting himself instead with a moral judgment on their role in enforcing the state's law. In any event, by authorizing "an action at law, suit in equity, *or other proper proceeding* for redress," Section 1983 opens the door to a distinction between an action for damages for past behavior and a suit to eliminate segregation in the future. It does not stretch the meaning of "proper proceeding for redress" to suggest that the phrase allows (or requires) the courts to grant "appropriate" remedies and to refuse to grant inappropriate ones, no matter how heinous the defendant's misconduct. If entrusted by Section 1983 with discretion, then, a court might order the members of a school board to take affirmative action for the future but hesitate to award damages for the past.

Some light is shed on this question by Section 1983's criminal-law counterpart, Section 242 of Title 18 of the United States Code, which provides that the willful deprivation of a person's federal rights under color of state law is a crime, punishable by fine, imprisonment, or both.[40] In a landmark case, *Screws v. United States,* the Supreme Court upheld the conviction of three Georgia police officers under this statute for their participation in a revolting episode in law enforcement, described as follows in Justice William O. Douglas' opinion:

> Petitioner Screws was sheriff of Baker County, Georgia. He enlisted the assistance of petitioner Jones, a policeman, and petitioner Kelley, a special deputy, in arresting Robert Hall, a citizen of the United States and of Georgia. The arrest was made late at night at Hall's home on a warrant charging Hall with theft of a tire. Hall, a young negro about thirty years of age, was handcuffed and taken by car to the court house. As Hall alighted from the car at the courthouse square, the three petitioners began beating him with their fists and with a solid-bar blackjack about eight inches long and weighing two pounds. They claimed Hall had reached for a gun and had used insulting language as he alighted from the car. But after Hall, still handcuffed, had been knocked to the ground they continued to beat him from fifteen to thirty minutes until he was unconscious. Hall was then dragged feet first through the court-house yard into the jail and thrown upon the floor dying. An ambulance was called and Hall was removed to a hospital where he died within the hour and

without regaining consciousness. There was evidence that Screws held a grudge against Hall and had threatened to "get" him.[41]

The principal legal argument advanced by the defendants was that the central operative phrase of Section 242—"willfully subjects [the victim] to the deprivation of any rights . . . secured or protected by the Constitution or laws of the United States"—was too vague for a criminal statute. Only a student of the Supreme Court's decisions, it was argued, could know when official conduct violates the Constitution, and even the most sedulous legal scholar might at times fail to foresee its interpretations in an unsettled area of constitutional law. For example, when the Supreme Court held that children cannot be required to recite a prayer or salute the flag in a public school in violation of their religious beliefs, could the teachers who had followed the contrary practice in a good-faith belief that it was permissible have been prosecuted under Section 242 for subjecting their students to a deprivation of their constitutional rights? The Supreme Court answered this question by holding in the *Screws* case that Section 242 applies only if the defendant acts "in open defiance or in reckless disregard of a constitutional requirement which has been made specific and definite," so that his conduct exhibits "a specific intent to deprive a person of a federal right made definite by decision or other rule of law." Later decisions have echoed this theme, and the criminal sanctions of Section 242 have been invoked primarily to punish the excessive use of physical force by police and prison officials.

In contrast to Section 242, Section 1983 imposes civil rather than criminal liability, and it does not require that the defendant act "willfully" in depriving the plaintiff of his federal rights. For these reasons, the Supreme Court refused in *Monroe v. Pape* to read into Section 1983 the requirement of a "specific intent" that it had previously imposed on Section 242. Instead, according to the Court, Section 1983 "should be read against the background of tort liability that makes a man responsible for the natural consequences of his actions."[42] By refusing to require a showing of evil intent, did the Supreme Court decide in effect that public officials can be held liable for civil damages under Section 1983 even if they were not warned in advance and had no other reason to suspect that their conduct would invade the plaintiff's federal rights? Is an official liable under Section 1983 for the faithful discharge of his duties under state law if it turns out that the law violates the federal Constitution or statutes—if, for example, he participated in administering a segregated school system before 1954?

We may be assisted in answering this question by examining still another Supreme Court decision, *Pierson v. Ray,* involving the applicability of Section 1983 itself. Three Mississippi police officers arrested a group of white and black clergymen in 1961 while they were attempting to use the segregated facilities at an interstate bus terminal in Jackson, Mississippi. The arrests were based on a Mississippi law providing that persons who congregate under circumstances that might lead to a breach of the peace are guilty of a misdemeanor if they refuse to comply with a police order to disperse. The clergymen were found guilty and sentenced to jail by a municipal judge, but on appeal one of them was acquitted and the charges against the others were dropped.

Four years later, in an unrelated case, the same breach-of-the-peace statute was held unconstitutional when applied to persons who were themselves peaceful, even though their defiance of local segregation practices might have inflamed a crowd of angry bystanders. In reliance on this decision, the clergymen in *Pierson v. Ray* sued the police officers who had arrested them, alleging that the arrests and ensuing jail sentences constituted a deprivation of their federal rights to use the bus station's facilities without regard to their race. The policemen responded that the arrests were made in good faith and with probable cause under a statute that they then believed to be valid, even if in the light of hindsight they were wrong. The Court upheld this defense, holding that Section 1983 should be interpreted in the context of accepted tort law:

> Under the prevailing view in this country a peace officer who arrests someone with probable cause is not liable for false arrest simply because the innocence of the suspect is later proved. . . . A policeman's lot is not so unhappy that he must choose between being charged with dereliction of duty if he does not arrest when he has probable cause, and being mulcted in damages if he does. Although the matter is not entirely free from doubt, the same consideration would seem to require excusing him from liability for acting under a statute that he reasonably believed to be valid but that was later held unconstitutional on its face or as applied.[43]

Having interpreted Section 1983 in this manner, the Court remanded the clergymen's case for a new trial, in which evidence to support or rebut the defenses of good faith and probable cause could be introduced. In returning the case for a second trial, the Court implied that if the trial court or jury believed that the purpose of the arrests was to enforce the custom of segregation rather than to prevent violence, the officers' defense of "good faith" and "probable cause" would fail. At bottom, then, the officers in *Pierson v. Ray* were held by the Supreme Court to be embraced by Section 1983 if they knowingly wielded the authority of the state to maintain segregated facilities in their community. One would have to be blind to the realities of our legal system to think that they were in grave jeopardy on the retrial.⁴⁴ At the same time, *Pierson v. Ray* suggests that a rudimentary reparations system might emerge from Section 1983, given proof that segregated facilities were maintained in defiance of federal constitutional requirements.

The rub in applying *Pierson v. Ray* to the lawsuit by my pupil whose assignment to a segregated school was held unconstitutional is that the injury occurred before the school board had any reason to believe that segregation was legally improper. Thus, its members would be excused for acting "under a statute that [they] reasonably believed to be valid but that was later held unconstitutional," unlike the police officers in *Pierson v. Ray,* who were accused of enforcing segregation in 1961, when its legal impropriety was manifest. The cases would be more comparable if the defendant in my hypothetical lawsuit was a school board that continued to segregate its pupils after 1954.

It should be pointed out, however, that the board's defense of "good faith," based on its pre-1954 belief that segregation was constitutionally permissible, ultimately rests on the Supreme Court's 1896 decision in *Plessy v. Ferguson,* which permitted the maintenance of segregated facilities only if, though "separate," they were "equal."⁴⁵

Though buried for years, this requirement of "equality" was resurrected by the courts in the nineteen-thirties and forties. In an all-but-forgotten campaign, the National Association for the Advancement of Colored People sought in numerous lawsuits to compel Southern school boards to supply black children with "equal" facilities as a condition of maintaining separate schools.⁴⁶

This prelude to *Brown v. Board of Education*—prelude

because it laid the groundwork for the decision in *Brown* that the intangible qualities of education cannot be equalized in a segregated system—included attacks by the NAACP on the inferior buildings, smaller per-student budgets, shorter school hours and semesters, limited curricula, and untrained teachers that were endemic to Negro schools in the South. In case after case, the federal courts warned that equality was a condition to separation; and if the NAACP's not inconsequential victories seem minor in retrospect, this is because the task of equalizing merely the physical facilities of the two school systems, let alone their other characteristics, was monumental.

My concern here is not to assess or even to describe the NAACP's campaign in full detail, but rather to argue that if Section 1983 required a warning to state officials that their pre-1954 conduct violated the federal constitutional standard, the course of decisions in this litigation should have been warning enough that segregated educational facilities for black children, in almost all areas and in almost all respects, were not "equal," and hence were not validated by the "separate but equal" formula of *Plessy v. Ferguson.* The NAACP's complaints were not cryptic or technical; the litigation was not conducted behind closed doors nor was the press excluded; the judicial opinions were not issued under a seal of secrecy. State officials may have shrugged the whole ruckus off, or blamed it on carpetbaggers or Communists, but that is merely to say that the warning was disregarded. Even in the criminal area the requirement of a "willful" violation of the victim's federal rights means "no more than intent without justification to bring about the circumstances which infringe [federal] rights."[47] As for civil liability, which routinely rests on such indefinite standards as "reasonable care" and "ordinary prudence," the course of litigation just described surely gave adequate notice to public officials that segregated facilities were tolerable only if there was a serious effort to make them "equal" as well as separate. It appears, therefore, that Section 1983 provides some support for my hypothetical lawsuit for damages resulting from pre-1954 school segregation if inequality in facilities can be adequately proved.

At first blush, a suit by a pupil who was compelled to attend a segregated school *after 1954*, in disregard of the Supreme Court's decision in *Brown v. Board of Education*, seems to be covered by *Pierson v. Ray* in that the school board is accused of preserving segregation with full knowledge of its constitutional invalidity. A transfer of the doctrine of *Pierson v. Ray* to the maintenance of segregated schools, however, encounters a problem that was not present in *Pierson v. Ray* itself. That case concerned an alleged attempt to perpetuate segregation in Jackson's interstate bus terminal, where immediate compliance with the principle of desegregation was feasible and to be expected. By contrast, the members of school boards may have been deluded, at least for a time, into thinking that school segregation could be preserved as a matter of local option, since many governors and leaders of the bar were busily spouting wishful theories in protest against *Brown v. Board of Education*. Even allowing for a waiting period for these notions of legal defiance to dissipate, however, the time is long past when even the most gullible public official can accept his governor's rhetorical assurance that *Brown v. Board of Education* is not the law of the land.

More troublesome—for its bearing on the "good faith" of a school board's members—is the argument that a segregated school system did not violate the federal rights of students, so far as damages under Section 1983 are concerned, until a reasonable time after the *Brown* decision. This argument would build on the Supreme Court's mandate in the *Brown* case, which did not order the defendant school boards to admit the plaintiff school children immediately, but rather required them to make "a prompt and reasonable start toward full compliance" and to justify any delay thereafter by showing that additional time "is necessary in the public interest and is consistent with good faith compliance at the earliest practicable date." This process was to be supervised by the federal district courts, which were instructed by the Supreme Court to insure the admission of the plaintiffs to the public school system on a racially nondiscriminatory basis "with all deliberate speed."[48]

Against this background, a school official who is sued under Section 1983 could argue that the assignment of a pupil to a segregated school after 1954 did not violate his federal rights if the dual system was being phased out with reasonable speed. Indeed, the official might assert more broadly that a local school board has no duty to act until a pupil in its own jurisdiction who has been assigned to a segregated school demands that he be reassigned on a nondiscriminatory basis. Only upon receiving a complaint, he might argue, would the board become obligated to eliminate segregation in the schools under its aegis; and even then, its duty would be to proceed "with all deliberate speed, not full speed ahead."[49]

To be sure, without a lawsuit a school board will not become subject to a judicial decree, and this absence of judicial guidance may enlarge the board's discretion in determining when to institute a plan of desegregation, what its scope should be, and how fast to move. Moreover, if there is no decree, the board cannot be punished for contempt of court, no matter how sluggish it may be. This, however, does not necessarily imply that the board can properly sit tight until it has been sued. A public official's obligation to uphold the Constitution encompasses the Supreme Court's interpretations of the Constitution, at least in the absence of evidence that they are obsolete and fated for retirement. In harmony with this view, the Supreme Court recently referred to a school board's "affirmative duty" to abandon segregation, describing its delay from 1954 until it was sued in 1965 as a "deliberate perpetuation of the unconstitutional dual system."[50] Besides implying quite clearly that school boards may not properly wait for students and their parents to complain, the Supreme Court has finally abandoned its tolerance of transitional delay, embodied in the "all deliberate speed" formula, by announcing that action must be taken "forthwith" to dismantle all remaining dual school systems.[51]

Moreover, even if the school board's obligation to convert to a unitary school system did not arise when the *Brown* case was decided but only at some later time, the pupils need not be denied damages for the inferior education they receive in the interim. In the *Brown* case, the Supreme Court exercised its equity power to allow school boards a reasonable time to conform to its decision; but it would not be inconsistent with this dispensation to require them to compensate those who are injured by the delay. Elsewhere in the law, when a party at fault asks for an extension of time to comply with the law, courts often grant the application only on condition that innocent persons be compensated for injuries suffered while waiting for the corrective action to be taken. If a factory pollutes a farmer's field, a court might well allow a reasonable time for the installation of pollution-control equipment, but require damages to be paid in the interim.

Section 1983, is applicable, of course, only if the plaintiff's federal rights have been violated. In granting school boards a reasonable period of time to convert to a unitary system, however, the Court did not retract or even qualify its view that the plaintiff's rights are violated by a dual school system. It merely announced that a particular species of relief —the extirpation of segregation—might require a period of adjustment and that this would justify postponing the day when the pupils could attend a desegregated school. This dispensation says nothing about the propriety of another form of relief, viz., pecuniary damages for the injury suffered by them in the meantime.

To summarize: *Monroe v. Pape* clearly acknowledged that public officials may be liable for damages under Section 1983 if, in faithfully discharging their duties under a state statute, they deprived the plaintiff of his federal constitutional rights, even if they did not have the type of "specific intent" to invade the victim's federal rights required for a criminal conviction under Section 242 of Title 18. But state and local officials cannot be held liable under Section 1983 for every act that is ultimately held to be improper under the Constitution; some play in the joints must be tolerated. Applied to the maintenance of segregated school facilities, this probably means that Section 1983 requires something akin to bad faith, contumacy, or wanton disregard of the school board's constitutional obligations. This element might be inferred from proof that even before a duty to desegregate arose, the board deliberately kept its all-black schools in a status of inequality in violation of the "separate but equal" doctrine, or that the board thereafter dragged its heels more stubbornly than the *Brown* case and its progeny permitted. For the first few years after *Brown* was decided, a school board might have been justified in waiting for its ramifications to be clarified. By now, however, a board that has not already made some progress in desegregating its facilities should not expect much tolerance for the defense that without a judicially pre-scribed timetable it could not figure out when it was required to start moving. This is why a rudimentary reparations pro-gram might emerge from Section 1983.

5.

The Status of Governmental Agencies under Section 1983

In discussing suits under Section 1983 for damages caused by the maintenance of a segregated school system, we must distinguish between, on the one hand, the liability of local school boards and other public agencies in their corporate capacity, and on the other, the personal liability of their individual members. The distinction is important because a judgment against a state agency will be paid out of public funds, while a judgment against a public official as an individual can be collected only from his private assets, unless the state has agreed to indemnify or insure him against such liabilities.[52] Moreover, solicitude for the defendant's pocketbook, given the fact that he was carrying out a public function approved by the public's duly elected representatives, will almost certainly lead juries to bend in his favor in individual cases, and may also lead, at the expense of plaintiffs, to legal presumptions and rules of a more general character

49

favoring defendants in such cases. For these reasons, it is necessary to examine whether Section 1983 imposes liability for damages on public agencies or only on their members.

In imposing liability on "every person" whose conduct under color of state law deprives another person of his federally protected rights, does Section 1983 reach only natural persons, or does the phrase "every person" also embrace state governments and their political subdivisions and administrative agencies? In the so-called Dictionary Act of the United States Code, some of the words and phrases used by Congress in statutes are defined and its definition of "person" is relevant here:

> [T]he word "person" may extend and be applied to bodies politic and corporate . . . unless the context shows that [it was] intended to be used in a more limited sense.[53]

This presumptively broad meaning of "person" takes on special weight when one realizes that the Dictionary Act was passed by Congress less than two months before it enacted Section 1983. (The dates are February 25 and April 20, 1871.) The draftsmen of statutes might become careless in time as the Dictionary Act receded into the background, but one would expect the Congressmen who enacted it to be quite explicit in using the term "person" if it was "intended to be used in a more limited sense." There is nothing explicit in the Ku Klux Act itself, however, to suggest that cities and states are not embraced by the language "every person," and it is clear that business corporations are potential defendants under Section 1983.[54]

Despite this, the Supreme Court held in *Monroe v. Pape* that the City of Chicago was not within the scope of the phrase "every person."[55] The only evidence cited by the Court for this narrow reading came not from Section 1983

itself but from the legislative history of a rejected amendment (the so-called Sherman Amendment) to another part
of the bill that became the Ku Klux Act. This amendment, providing that persons injured by a racially motivated riot or tumultuous assembly could recover full compensation from the inhabitants of the city or county in
which the offense was committed, was adopted by the
Senate but rejected by the House of Representatives. A
revised version, placing the liability directly on the cities
and counties as political bodies rather than on their inhabitants, was also rejected by the House. A substitute,
which is now Section 1986 of Title 42, was then adopted,
attacking the problem in a more limited fashion by imposing liability on any person who, having the power to
prevent certain infringements of civil rights, fails to act
with reasonable diligence to prevent their commission.

The House of Representatives rejected the broader proposal to make cities and counties liable for damages inflicted
by racially motivated riots because, according to a spokesman for the House conference,

> Congress had no constitutional power to impose any obligation
> upon county and town organizations, the mere instrumentality
> for the administration of State law.[56]

The Supreme Court in *Monroe v. Pape* moved quickly from
this explanation of the House's rejection of the Sherman
Amendment to the conclusion that Section 1983 does not
impose liability on municipalities.

This conclusion, however, does not flow so easily from the
premise. Although the legislative history is not free from
doubt, the constitutional objection to the Sherman Amendment was seemingly based not on the broad claim that all
state agencies are totally immune to federal authority, but on

a narrower theory, viz., an alleged lack of federal power over the distribution of governmental authority *within* a state. It should be remembered that the rejected proposal imposed liability on cities and counties whether or not they were vested under state law with the police power to prevent riots and unlawful assemblies. This led one of the opponents of the Sherman Amendment to point out that whatever may have been the customary powers of cities, counties ordinarily "do not have control of the police affairs of the county and the administration of justice." He went on to say:

> Hence it seems to me that these provisions attempt to impose obligations upon a county for the protection of life and person which are not imposed by the laws of the State, and that it is beyond the power of the General [i.e., national] Government to require their performance.

Although he did not cite a specific constitutional provision, his theory may have been that control over the distribution of powers within each state is "reserved to the States" by the Tenth Amendment, and that a federal law imposing liability on counties or cities (rather than on the states themselves) was an improper interference with a state's distribution of local authority.

Had it dealt only with the improper exercise of powers *actually* granted by a state to its cities and counties, the Sherman Amendment's constitutional validity might well have been viewed differently. Indeed, the same opponent of the Sherman Amendment conceded that "where the equal protection required to be afforded by a State is imposed upon a city *by State laws,* perhaps the United States courts *could* enforce its performance."[57] *Monroe v. Pape* held that Section 1983 imposes liability on public officials who violate federal rights in administering state authority vested in them by the state. It would be possible to hold cities and counties liable under Section 1983 for the improper discharge of *their* state-granted powers without undercutting the result in *Monroe v. Pape,* though part of its reasoning would have to give way. The phrase "every person" in Section 1983 could be construed to include subordinate political agencies without simultaneously making them responsible for the unauthorized acts of their employees. The police officers in that case were not acting in conformity to their official instructions; although this did not preclude personal liability under Section 1983, it would not necessarily serve to impose liability on the city unless it had encouraged or condoned their misconduct.

All this leads me to suggest that the citadel of municipal immunity created by *Monroe v. Pape* may not be impregnable, and that the term "every person" in Section 1983 may in time be construed in the broader sense sanctioned by the 1871 Dictionary Act: to include all "bodies politic."[58] I would offer in support of this prediction not only the legislative history just described but also some of the curious results of granting immunity to cities and counties.

Thus, a question that has perplexed the courts in interpreting Section 1983 is whether it applies to private persons; the answer turns on whether persons who do not hold public office may be said to act "under color" of state law, a prerequisite to liability under Section 1983. The Supreme Court's response to this question, after many false starts and with continuing disagreement, has been that private persons act "under color" of state law when they act in cahoots with public officials or when they are, or think they are, compelled to act in an improper fashion by state law.[59] The significance of this struggle over the inclusion of private persons in the ambit of Section 1983 is that its applicability to public agencies would have seemed—prior to *Monroe v. Pape*—to be an easier case.

The same conclusion might have been inferred from the Supreme Court's answer to another perplexing issue under Section 1983 and its criminal-law counterpart (Section 242 of Title 18), viz., the status of a public official whose misconduct violates state as well as federal law. If, in depriving someone of a right secured by the Constitution or laws of the United States, the official contravenes the state laws and regulations that are supposed to govern his behavior, can he be said to act "under color" of state law? As pointed out earlier, some judges persistently answered this question in the negative; but it is by now well established that the official's misconduct constitutes action under color of state law even if he is faithless to his oath of office. If this is so—and here again I refer to ground already covered—it is an easier case to hold that an official who does just what state law required of him is acting under color of state law. And if the faithful public official can be held liable under Section 1983 when the statute under which he is operating is unconstitutional,[60] it would be odd to exonerate his employer from concurrent liability.

Whether or not the Supreme Court sees fit at some future time to reexamine its determination in *Monroe v. Pape* that cities are not subject to liability under Section 1983, it is of major importance that the holding did not confer immunity upon the state itself but only on its political subdivisions. If we are right in asserting that the crux of the constitutional objection to the Sherman Amendment was that it interfered with the distribution of powers *within states* by imposing liability on political subdivisions that might not have been vested with the police power by the state, it follows that the imposition of liability *on the state itself* stands on a different footing. One of the opponents of the Sherman Amendment came close to making this very point:

> But I doubt the constitutionality of the amendment. This General Government, as I understand it, deals with States and with citizens. It does not know such things as towns, parishes, and counties. They are the integral parts of States; they are entirely under the government of the States as political corporations, and the Constitution of the United States recognizes no relation between the Federal Government and these subordinate political corporations.[61]

Another was even more explicit:

> I hold that this duty of protection, if it rests anywhere, rests on the State, and that if there is to be any liability visited upon anybody for a failure to perform that duty, such liability should be brought home to the State. Hence, in my judgment, this section would be liable to very much less objection, both in regard to its justice and its constitutionality, if it provided that if in any State the offenses named in this section were committed, suit might be brought against the State, judgment obtained, and payment of the judgment might be enforced upon the treasury of the State.[62]

Thus, the evidence—indirect at best—used by the Supreme Court in *Monroe v. Pape* to rebut the normally broad meaning of "every person" in Section 1983 suggests, at most, a doubt about the power of Congress to impose civil liability on cities, counties, and other subordinate agencies of the state. But rather than implying a parallel doubt about imposing liability on the states themselves, it suggests the absence of any scruple on this point. When Congress used the term "every person" in Section 1983, two months after saying in the Dictionary Act that the term "person" included "bodies politic and corporate" unless the context indicated a narrower reach, it did not exhibit an intent to exclude states. We can conclude, therefore, that the immunity granted by *Monroe v. Pape* to municipal corporations does not necessarily extend to the state itself, though it must be admitted that there is weighty authority to the contrary.[63]

Assuming the possibility of damage suits against the state or its agencies under Section 1983, one must come to grips with a secondary argument, advanced in *Monroe v. Pape* by the City of Chicago but left unanswered as moot when complete municipal immunity was granted by the Court. This argument was that Section 1983 should be interpreted to exempt public bodies from liability for violations of civil rights in the discharge of such essential governmental functions as the provision of police protection. Section 1983 itself, of course, does not explicitly immunize any public functions from liability, but the Supreme Court on several occasions had held that certain exemptions found in the common law of tort liability should be read into Section 1983. Thus, the policemen who were sued in *Pierson v. Ray* were permitted to interpose the defense of good faith and probable cause for their otherwise improper arrests of the protesting clergymen; there is no explicit hint of such a defense in the language of Section 1983. *Pierson v. Ray* also held that liability could not be imposed under Section 1983 on the judges who had tried and convicted the plaintiffs, because the Court did not think that Congress in enacting Section 1983 intended to abandon the general tort-law principle of absolute immunity for judicial behavior.[64] Another instance of the preservation of tort law under Section 1983 is *Tenney v. Brandhove,* involving allegations that a fact-finding committee on un-American activities established by the California State Senate had infringed the plaintiff's federal civil rights by conducting a hearing and instigating criminal proceedings against him in retaliation for his attempt to get the state legislature to cut the committee's appropriations. Holding that his complaint was properly dismissed by the district court, the Supreme Court read into Section 1983 an implied absolute exemption from civil liability for legislators acting within the sphere of their legislative activity.[65] Although the point was not mentioned by the Court in the *Tenney* case, it is interesting to recall that in 1871 one of the Congressmen opposing the enactment of Section 1983 predicted that it would impose liability on legislators who voted for an unconstitutional law —his example was a state law providing for segregated schools!—and on any state court judges who enforced it.[66]

These instances, based on the common law, of implied immunity from liability under Section 1983 have deep roots in the English struggle for Parliamentary and judicial independence of the Crown, and in the conviction that public officials should not be held personally accountable for errors when they act in good faith and with probable cause. But if these decisions were extended to immunize all governmental behavior in the conduct of essential governmental functions, as was asked by the City of Chicago in *Monroe v. Pape*, the only remaining area for public liability under Section 1983 would be such occasional and relatively trivial "proprietary" activities as the conduct of a business for profit.[67]

If the courts can bring themselves to accept the argument made earlier in favor of governmental liability under Section 1983, they ought to construe the coverage generously rather than simultaneously undercutting its scope by immunizing essential governmental functions. Applied to *future* action, to be sure, such a restriction would be of only minor importance. Since the courts can "restrain individual state officers from doing what the 14th Amendment forbids the State to do,"[68] impose fines or jail sentences if they violate the order, and renew the order against their successors if they resign, future behavior can be brought under effective judicial control. Where damages for past misconduct are at stake, however, to remit the plaintiff to an action against individual officials would have the consequence, mentioned earlier, of denying an effective remedy if they are impecunious. At most, the "essential governmental function" exemption ought to go no farther than to relieve the state from vicarious liability for the unauthorized torts of its employees. This would give the exemption its fullest appropriate scope, i.e., to avoid interference with essential functions when an incidental error is committed in administration. There is no sound reason for extending it to ordinary governmental functions, however "essential," that are deliberately operated in a fashion violating the citizen's civil rights.

6.

The Measurement of Damages for Segregation in Public Facilities

Justice Harlan asked in *Monroe v. Pape,* "[W]hat is the dollar value of the right to go to unsegregated schools?"[69] Conversely, what is the pecuniary loss that results from compulsory attendance at a segregated school? Like the discussion of liability, these comments on damages are not primarily concerned solely with the technical possibility of using Section 1983 as the base for a system of reparations. Rather, they are intended to suggest that any proposal for reparations—whether narrowly or broadly conceived, whether funded by public or private agencies—must come to grips with a series of subordinate issues, one of which is the measurement of damages. Section 1983 is a suggestive analogy, rather than a prototype to be accepted or rejected without change.

It is obviously a formidable task to ascertain the damages that result from compulsory attendance at a segregated school, whether or not its physical facilities are equal to the parallel white school. Before concluding that the task is impossible, however, we should remind ourselves that our courts spend much of their time on automobile-accident cases in which the loss of earnings and earning capacity, as well as emotional distress and similar imponderables, are routinely converted into dollars. Though it is difficult and often distasteful to transmute precious things into base metal, few would argue that the effort should be abandoned. Doing something is not always better than standing still, but an educated guess may be better than refusing to make any estimate at all, which is the functional equivalent of estimating the damages at zero.

It would be possible, for example, to start with the substantial body of information now available about the comparative earnings of black and white employees of the same age, and to attribute all or a reasonable part of the gap— about $1,500 per person per year in 1969[70]—to differences in educational opportunities. The disparity could be refined by filtering out the effects of geography, and if culture-free tests of aptitude and intelligence become available, these characteristics could also be eliminated in estimating the reduction in earning capacity resulting from educational handicaps. Aid in measuring the economic effects of segregated schools might also be derived from a comparison of the wage history of blacks graduating from such schools with those of blacks graduating from integrated schools. A similar comparison is sanctioned by the courts in assessing damages when a child's earning capacity is depressed or destroyed by an automobile accident or other wrongful injury. Rather than denying any recovery because the "true" damages cannot be computed with assurance, evidence of the average earnings of similarly situated persons is admitted to establish what the child, no matter how young, would probably have earned during a normal lifetime if his faculties had not been wrongfully damaged.[71] Another example: in a recent case involving discrimination in employment opportunities practiced by a labor union, the court awarded as damages the difference between the average earnings of union members and the lesser amount earned by comparable black members.[72] In a similar vein, the German plan for compensating victims of Nazi persecution included pensions to civil servants and military personnel who were dismissed from their posts, the level of benefits being calculated on the assumption that the claimant would have remained in his chosen occupation for an average lifetime, with a normal number of promotions and pay increases.

The disparity in earnings between blacks and whites of equal potential is made more painful by the emotional injury inflicted by racial discrimination. In its reparations program, Germany provided compensation for the psychic injury produced by such practices as excluding Jews from places of public accommodation and requiring them to wear a yellow armband or the Star of David as an invitation to private discrimination. It is difficult to convert humiliation and emotional distress into cash, but American courts regularly rise to the challenge by compensating the victims of slanderous utterances, abusive tactics by bill collectors, misdelivery of telegraphic notices of illness or death, insults by hotel employees, interferences with burials, invasions of privacy, unjustified picketing of personal residences, wrongful sexual advances, and innumerable other acts causing mental distress but no visible physical injury. Such recoveries are not unknown in the area of racial practices: there is a long line of cases holding Southern railroads liable for assigning white passengers to Jim Crow cars; a Negro was recently awarded damages for the psychological trauma suffered when a land-lord refused to rent him an apartment because of his race; and a prisoner who was wrongfully held in solitary confinement ("punitive segregation") was awarded damages of $9,300 (calculated at the rate of $25 per day) in a Section 1983 suit against the warden.[73]

For want of a better measure of these imponderables, we might speculate about the outcome of a lawsuit for damages brought by a white pupil who was erroneously assigned to a Jim Crow school for a school year before *Brown v. Board of Education* was decided. Disregarding extraneous defenses such as sovereign immunity, I venture the guess that a Southern jury would be more likely to award damages of $25,000 rather than $1,000. (Without wishing to overemphasize it, I offer as a bit of relevant evidence a $875 jury award in 1913 to a white railroad passenger for being compelled to ride for three miles in a Jim Crow car.)[74] Altering the facts of the hypothetical lawsuit to assume that a black pupil erroneously assigned to a white school had sued for damages (and assuming that he was not held in contempt of court for impudence in claiming any injury at all), I suggest that the damages would have been closer to $1,000 than to $25,000. The difference between the recoveries could be regarded as the community's assessment of the "cost" of being black. The comparison is, of course, faulty in that the impact on a white child of a year in a segregated black school is not the same as the impact of a year in the same school on a black child. Given a segregated society, the white child may feel isolated or abandoned, while the black child may feel protected.[75] On the other hand, the white child knows that his assignment is a mistake and that it will be corrected. He resembles the mythical prince who is exiled by a wicked stepfather but remains confident of reinstatement; by contrast, the black child in the same society knows that his assigned status is permanent. One can test this suggestion by imagining that the white child and his parents are swarthy newcomers, whose racial derivation is being debated by the neighbors, and that the school board's decision, though reversed a year later, leaves a lingering doubt in the community about whether they are "really" white. However much this comparison may be discounted, I think it contains a core of realism: assignment to a black school system was an injury for which, applying the standards customarily used in Anglo-American law to quantify the imponderable, substantial damages would be appropriate.

A technique that might be borrowed from tort law to assist in measuring damages for humiliation is the "per diem" method, sanctioned by some courts, which consists of instructing the jury to make an initial estimate of damages for one day of physical pain or emotional distress, and then to multiply this amount by the number of days of suffering. This is not the place for a comprehensive examination or even a survey of the measurement of damages for humiliation and mental suffering. It is enough to acknowledge that traditional legal doctrines and mechanisms have been able to compensate for such injuries in resolving specific disputes in many areas of human activity, and that there is no reason to believe that a systematic refusal to place a price tag on this type of injury would be better than the estimates, crude as they are, that the courts in fact impose on the parties.

It is, of course, familiar knowledge that the economic and social status of blacks is depressed by a combination of factors, of which unequal educational opportunity is only one. The others include segregation in all of its other aspects as well as private discriminatory behavior. However, if the states themselves are not within the reach of Section 1983, so that damages can be imposed under Section 1983 only on the public officials who administer unconstitutional state laws, a troublesome problem of allocation arises. On this reading of the statute, school officials would be liable only for the economic injury attributable to their agencies, and the superintendents of public buildings and other places of public accommodation would be liable only for damages resulting from segregation in their facilities, and so on. This might permit the attribution of an ascertainable share of the responsibility for the impaired earning capacity of blacks to the school system, though the problem of measurement would be formidable. Agencies whose link to earning capacity is more attenuated, however, might be held responsible only for the direct results of specific acts of exclusion or discrimination and not for their unmeasurable contribution to the economic status of blacks in the society.

If an allocation of responsibility for the Negro's depressed economic status among the many contributing state agencies is required by Section 1983, the division will at best be artificial; at worst, it may be so hopelessly unpersuasive that an action against the members of a school board or other agency will be dismissed for failure to carry the burden of proof, a burden that always falls on the plaintiff in a lawsuit. If, however, Section 1983 is construed (as suggested earlier) to impose liability on the state itself rather than solely on the public officials who administer unconstitutional state statutes, this difficulty might evaporate, since much if not all of the economic injury resulting from these diverse sources could be properly attributed to action by the state as the ultimate source of authority for the conduct of all its subordinate agencies and instrumentalities. This would surely be an appropriate response to a claim that along with the dual school system, segregated facilities in parks, libraries, recreational areas, and public buildings contributed to the injury. Section 1983 might also be construed to impose pecuniary liability on the state for discrimination by privately owned facilities, such as restaurants, hotels, theaters, buses, and railroad stations, that were segregated under compulsion of state law. Finally, without going so far as to assert that all private discrimination was state-inspired, segregation in such large-scale institutions as major industries and labor unions (which are aided and regulated by a dense network of state law) was sufficiently encouraged or buttressed by state action to generate state liability for damages under Section 1983.[76]

If accepted, this concept of unitary state liability would culminate in a single judgment under Section 1983 against the state. It would not be necessary to allocate the responsibility for the pecuniary damages among the subordinate agencies in proportion to their separate contributions to the resulting injury, since the state itself stands behind these diverse forces, whether they be inferior educational opportunities, segregated public facilities, or compulsory discrimination in places of public accommodation. While it would be theoretically appropriate to exonerate the state from liability for damages clearly attributable to private behavior that was unaffected by state compulsion, provocation, or encouragement, it would be at least equally reasonable to exclude evidence of so speculative a defense. The same response would be appropriate to the similar defense that other states contributed to the aggregate injury, either because the plaintiff was a migrant or because segregation in a neighboring state buttressed the local practices that injured the plaintiff. An analogy that comes to mind is the well-entrenched and frequently applied rule of admiralty law governing liability for collisions at sea, which provides that a ship that has violated a rule prescribing safety equipment or navigational procedures is responsible for all the resulting damage unless it establishes that its breach of the law could not, by any possibility, have contributed to the collision. The courts candidly acknowledge that this presumption of liability can rarely be rebutted in practice, but defend its draconic impact as an appropriate device to insure compliance with the statutory standards.[77]

It should be clear from this discussion that a system of reparations based on individual lawsuits would produce very diverse recoveries. If the fact-finding process is reliable, the remedy would reflect the evidence offered by each plaintiff of his own experience, so that he would be compensated in proportion to his own injury. But if the fact-finding process is unreliable, the tailor-made suit, though expensive to produce, might not fit. If individualization of the remedy is undesirable because the process would be ungainly to administer, or would produce haphazard results, or would be thought invidious by the recipients, a program of reparations could employ instead a predetermined schedule of amounts to be paid to claimants on the basis of such rough but objective criteria as age, occupation, and place of residence. Benefit schedules based on averages and taking minimal account of individual differences are familiar devices in our society; they are used to determine the amounts to be paid to veterans for service-connected disabilities, to workmen injured in the course of employment, to welfare clients, and to recipients of many other benefits. Section 1983 itself, however, embodies the traditional common-law approach to damages, treating each plaintiff as a discrete individual whose personal circumstances determine the amount of his recovery, without regard to what may be received by other potential plaintiffs for their injuries. This momentous choice between emulating Section 1983 and replacing it by a schedule of compensatory amounts will be examined in a later chapter.

7.

Section 1983: Epilogue

This examination of Section 1983 is not designed to establish that we now have a functioning system of black reparations. Its purpose, rather, is to suggest that this century-old
statute may permit, in circumstances whose hazy contours
would have to be clarified by protracted litigation, damage
actions for the injury caused by segregation in public schools
and other public facilities. Beyond that, Section 1983 is a
statutory springboard from which we could plunge into
deeper waters if the spirit moves us. A study of Section 1983
may also serve to reduce the emotional temperature that has
characterized the discussion of black reparations. Far from
being a bizarre, outrageous, and unprecedented proposal, it
turns out to be a concept that invites, and is susceptible to,
ordinary legal analysis. More than that, the demand for compensation has fraternal links with familiar legal doctrines
and institutions, links that are so numerous and so powerful

that the response "Why not?" might be more appropriate than "Why?"

Perhaps this point can be strengthened by asking whether, assuming the validity of my interpretation of Section 1983, the reader would favor its repeal. I am referring not to repeal because of deficiencies (e.g., the imposition of liability on individual public officials rather than on the state itself) that could be corrected by amending Section 1983, but repeal because the reader thinks it unfair to compensate persons who are injured by official conduct transgressing constitutional norms. The reader who is inclined in this direction might ask himself whether his objection to compensation embraces all official misconduct or only some categories, and if the latter, what distinguishes those that should be remedied by compensation from those that should be left to other modes of correction. Conversely, a judgment to preserve Section 1983, either intact or amended to bridge some gaps in its coverage, implies a willingness to compensate persons who have been injured by official misconduct. In short, I do not see how judgment can be passed on Section 1983 without thinking seriously about the concept of black reparations.

Section 1983 is a useful starting point not only for skeptics but also for proponents of black reparations, since it suggests a number of troublesome questions that must be answered if they hope to move from slogans to programs. Should compensation go to individuals, as is done under Section 1983, or to groups, as proposed by the Black Manifesto? If individuals are to be compensated, should the benefits be uniform for all recipients, or graduated according to each one's personal experience and circumstances? Will it be necessary to promulgate an official code of racial classification to administer a reparations program? If so, will the code create more problems than the reparations program will cure? Would a program of reparations exclusively for blacks be constitutional? Finally, where should a reparations program rank among the many other claims for public support? Will it divert funds that would otherwise be used to benefit the nation's poor, black and white alike? The rest of this book is devoted to an examination of these issues.

8.

Compensation to Groups or to Individuals?

I have already pointed out that Section 1983 can be invoked by a group of persons seeking injuctive relief (e.g., a court order directing a school board to cease and desist from assigning students on a racially discriminatory basis), but that when a money judgment is sought, it is every man for himself. To recover, a plaintiff must establish a deprivation of *his* rights and the extent of *his own* injury; a corollary of this requirement is that he is entitled to collect and retain any damages awarded to him in a successful legal action. By contrast, the $500 million of reparations demanded by the Black Manifesto was to be used to establish a Southern land bank, publishing companies, TV networks, research and training centers, an organization of welfare recipients, a black labor strike fund, a fund-raising organization, and a black university. There was no demand for direct compensation to individuals.

A program of group reparations would be profoundly different in its consequences from payments to individuals. The Black Manifesto used $15 per person as the base for its demand that the churches and synagogues pay an aggregate of $500 million to the designated institutions. Whether the per capita base is $15 or $15,000, however, the point is the same: if paid to individuals, the money would be used for groceries, automobiles, occupational training, lottery tickets, and mutual-fund shares. The same amount given to organizations would be used for group activities—education, publicity, the financing of businesses or cooperatives, research, and so on. The choice of objectives would thus be centralized rather than dispersed, and the directors, officials, and staff members of the organizations receiving the funds would enjoy the prerogatives and carry the burdens of management before their constituencies would receive the benefits. I do not mean that benefits are necessarily attenuated as they trickle down from organizations to their members, beneficiaries, and clients; to the contrary, they might have the advantage of being concentrated. But the choice of means and ends would be vested in a different, and smaller, group of hearts and minds. The managers and their organizations would be transformed overnight from voices crying in the wilderness into major social and political institutions.

To support the claim that they are the appropriate recipients of reparations, the organizations would no doubt assert that they are the "legitimate" representatives of the blacks of America. If they are, one might ask whether a program of direct compensation to individuals would be equally acceptable, since—assuming that the leaders do indeed enjoy the confidence claimed or at least implied by the Black Manifesto—their organizations would then receive voluntary contributions in proportion to the strength of this claim. The dynamics of institutional bureaucracy may be different among blacks than among whites, but I doubt it; and this leads me to suspect that organized groups would not be enthusiastic about a proposal that they rely on voluntary contributions from their constituents. There would be no hypocrisy in such a refusal to put the loyalty of their memberships to a financial test: fear that the common man will disregard his "best" or his "long-run" interests is endemic to all human institutions.

It may be argued, in support of proposals for group reparations to blacks, that this is a familiar American pattern for the resolution of Indian claims. Indeed, the jurisdiction of the Indian Claims Commission, established in 1946 to hear and determine claims against the United States, is restricted to claims presented "on behalf of any Indian tribe, band, or other identifiable group of American Indians." Under this provision a recognized tribal organization takes precedence over less well-defined groups, unless there is a showing of fraud or other impropriety on its part.[78] An Indian spokesman, Vine Deloria, Jr., has recently argued that this pattern of group representation is a suitable precedent for a program of black reparations:

> Taken together, all of the power movements and the emergence of the Woodstock Nation call for a renovation of state and federal laws on the basis of understanding the rights of groupings of people who have desires over and above the simple articulation of their individual rights. Thus the concept of "reparations" has recently come into existence in the black community. There is no simple answer for this demand since it speaks of payments due to the black community and not to any specific individual black for a specific wrong suffered. . . .
>
> In [regard to] Constitutional recognition of the rights of groups, Indian tribes are much further ahead than are other

groups. In 1946 the Indian Claims Commission was established to litigate outstanding claims that Indian tribes might have against the United States based on treaties and land cessions. This commission thus provides a prototype of structure by which the aspirations and claims of minority groups can be realized.[79]

To recognize the tribe as the proper recipient for Indian payments, however, is to accept the group's own loyalties and culture. This is illustrated not only by the refusal to make payments directly to individual Indians, but by the converse refusal to disregard their diverse (and sometimes adversary) tribal loyalties by treating them as a single homogenized people. This approach cannot be automatically transferred to black–white relations. The American descendants of such diverse African ethnic and tribal groups as the Ibo, Akan, Yoruba, Hausa, and Bantu, for example, do not maintain distinctive tribal organizations, official membership rolls, or comparable devices to protect their separate ancestral heritages from being blurred by intermarriage with each other. As a result, the tribal loyalties threatening the continued existence of some newly independent African nations seem to have had no echo in the communal life of American blacks. By contrast, American Indians, even in their worst days, were able to preserve the structure and emotional attachments that characterized their separate tribal organizations.

If the Indian tribe has any counterpart in the community life of American blacks, it is the idea of black solidarity. But the comparison is not, as of today, a compelling one. Despite increasing references to "the black experience" and exhortations to solidarity, even the most ardent supporters of black unity acknowledge that it is a goal, not an established institution. Among American blacks today, differences in economic status, geographical origin and current location, outlook, organizational ties, and educational background are powerful centrifugal forces that black nationalist groups have not succeeded in neutralizing. It is understandable that those who seek a more tightly organized people would favor group reparations and might view any reluctance to accept the premise of unity as an attempt to interfere with black self-determination. With greater accuracy, however, blacks who are skeptical or distrustful of institutionalized unity can assert that the sudden acceptance by the government of the concept of black unity would be a massive intrusion into the area of black organization—not a merely passive acceptance of the authentic wishes of American blacks.

As a precedent, then, for recognizing American blacks as a single people, the statutory requirement that the Indian Claims Commission deal only with Indian "tribes, bands, and other identifiable groups" is at best a weak analogy and at worst a misleading one. The lesson to be derived from the "Indian reparations" experience may be, rather, that the government should deal with either individuals or groups, depending on the preexisting organization of the recipients. This would imply that if American blacks have not already created something akin to a nation—one big tribe—the government ought to continue to treat them as individuals lest it coerce them into a community structure that does not command the loyalty that Indian tribal groupings have inherited and preserved.

In response to this contention, it may, of course, be asserted that white hostility has been more important than black self-determination in our history, and that if "black power" is only a rallying cry rather than an accurate description of an existing institution, this is because black ambitions have been actively thwarted by governmental and private practices. Had the white majority been neutral, perhaps the black minority would be more unified. Just as it is argued that compensation, rather than equality, is a necessary condition to the rectification of past inequalities, so it may be argued that governmental recognition of blacks as a group is an appropriate way to create the conditions that would now exist if neutrality and equality had been America's policy from the outset of black–white relations.

I would suggest, however, the contrary hypothesis: that equality and neutrality would have generated a level of assimilation in which black institutions would be even more fragmented than they now are. To be sure, we are now beginning to realize that ethnic loyalties survived the melting pot to a much greater degree than had been thought, and blacks would no doubt have survived integration even if it had been practiced consistently and enthusiastically ever since the adoption of the Fourteenth Amendment. But I find it difficult to believe that America's blacks would be a more cohesive society today—more like an Indian tribe—if white policies had been neutral rather than discriminatory. In the intellectual and social life of black Americans, the pendulum has swung back and forth between assimilationist and nationalist trends, frequently in response to internal black perceptions of the attitude of whites toward an integrated society. For the group life of its victims, discrimination is more likely to be a glue than a solvent.

In *We Talk, You Listen,* Deloria assails the practice of treating black–white relationships as the norm in discussions of social problems, with Indians being relegated to the category of "others" who are to ride along on the tail of the kite:

During the rise of the civil rights movement and its expansion into the power movements, Indian people were often derided for their refusal to participate in demonstrations and confrontations. Every time an activist discovered Indians, he was horrified to learn that they were not about to begin marching. Because they equated Indian problems with those of other groups, many people felt that if Indians used the same tactics which had worked with the black community, Indian problems could be solved. Everyone spoke of the spectacular results that other groups were having, and it became sociological heresy for Indians to refuse to imitate these other groups. . . . The whole field of relationships between the different groups in society has been perverted by failing to understand the necessity to change words and meanings when dealing with different groups. Thus "intergroup relations" has become synonymous with race relations, which means whites and blacks. . . .

The whole of American society has been brainwashed into believing that if it understood blacks it could automatically understand every other group simply because blacks were the most prominent minority group with which white society had to deal.[80]

Deloria's point is a powerful one, but it may be even more telling than he recognizes. While demanding that we cease "to view the world through traditional black–white glasses," he may have failed to notice the red-tinted spectacles that color his own vision. They may explain his conviction that "tribalization" is the remedy for America's social ills, without any regard for the history, self-perception, or ambitions of the social, ethnic, national, linguistic, geographic, and economic groups to whom he offers this advice. For those who are labeled "others" on Deloria's map of society, "tribalization" may be as countercultural as, according to him, "individualization" is to the American Indian. If so, the Indian Claims Commission's focus on the rights of "tribes, bands, and other identifiable groups of Indians" would be a poor model for a black reparations program, however suitable it may be for Indian claims. Though not conclusive on this point, an interesting fact about the Indian Claims Commission Act is that it does not cover claims for injuries to individuals, even if presented by their tribes, for "the general harm—psychological, social, cultural, economic—done the Indians by the historical national policy of semi-apartheid" and by federal failure to provide adequate education and medical care to individuals.[81]

Can the question of individual-versus-group payments be resolved for the black-reparations area by dividing the sum equally between individuals and organized groups? This solution might be hailed as the wisdom of Solomon, but more likely it would satisfy no one. To be sure, the German program of reparations to the Jewish victims of Nazi persecution included payments to the State of Israel and to an International Claims Conference (representing a broad spectrum of Jewish organizations outside Israel, and charged with responsibility for the relief, rehabilitation, and resettlement of non-Israeli Jews), as well as direct payments to individuals.[82] But Israel was included in the compensation program because it had borne the economic burden of resettling many refugees from Germany, and the Claims Conference was treated, in effect, as the residuary legatee of the Jews who had been exterminated along with their heirs in the Nazi holocaust. Because of these special features of the German reparations plan, its structure is not a compelling model for black reparations.

The choice between individual reparations and group payments is so momentous, and its resolution so likely to elicit charges of governmental meddling in the "internal" affairs of black recipients, that there is a temptation to think that the issue can be finessed by vesting the decision exclusively in the black victims of racial discrimination. A realistic examination of this route to neutrality, however, discloses that at best it will provide only a bit of camouflage, and at worst it may become an unexpected battlefield. This is because the entity that makes the payments—churches, government, or other institutions—must either decide the ultimate question or establish the rules by which it will be decided. Thus, if the churches had made payments to Forman's group, it would have been as much the nominee of the white churches as of the black masses it claimed to represent. The credibility and force of its demands, to be sure, depended on the support it was thought to have among America's blacks, or at least among their vocal and influential segments; but in the end, it would have been white perceptions, not black votes, that would have brought Forman's group to the center of the stage. This is equally true of the recommendation for a reparations commission made by the National Black Political Convention at its meeting in Gary, Indiana, in the spring of 1972:

> The economic impoverishment of the Black community in America is clearly traceable to the historic enslavement of our people and to the racist discrimination to which we have been subjected since "emancipation." Indeed, much of the unprecedented economic wealth and power of American capitalism has obviously been built upon this exploitation of Black people.
>
> Therefore, an incalculable social indebtedness has been generated, a debt which is owed to Black people by the general American society. So, while the moral horrors of slavery and the human indignities visited upon our people by racial discrimination can never really be compensated for—and certainly never with money alone—we must not rest until American society has recognized our valid, historic right to reparations, to a massive

claim on the financial assets of the American economy. At the same time, it is necessary Black people realize that full economic development for us cannot take place without radical transformation of the economic system which has so clearly exploited us these many years.

It is against the background of such realities that we move to a Black Agenda for economic empowerment.

RECOMMENDATION: That there be established a presidential commission, with a majority of Black members (chosen by the Black Convention or its successor body) to determine a procedure for calculating an appropriate reparations payment in terms of land, capital and cash and for exploring the ways in which the Black community prefers to have this payment implemented.[83]

Not even a verbatim acceptance of this proposal could obscure the fact that it inescapably depends on presidential action. By acting favorably on the recommendation, the President (rather than the black citizens of America) would necessarily be deciding that the National Black Political Convention is the appropriate body to nominate the black members of the proposed commission—in preference, for example, to the National Black Economic Development Conference or a specially convened new body of representatives.

To be blunt, a chosen instrument is a mercenary. This is obviously true of an organization that is selected because it has a tradition of complaisant adjustment to the wishes of the Establishment. It is also true of an organization whose "legitimacy" derives from its prior independence or militancy. It will be chosen only if that stance suits the government's purpose, and it will be retained only so long as it continues to serve that purpose.[84] What is involved is not the familiar practice of appointing a black, a Puerto Rican, a

Jew, and a Catholic to a commission on civil rights or human relations, or making an occasional government grant to foster racially oriented work by a black theater or studio, but the continuing responsibility for a large-scale program with a commitment of public funds so far greater as to be different in kind, not merely in degree. Co-optation, of course, may take longer in some cases than others; but we are talking about a program that will extend over a period of many years.

If those who are to make the payments refer the question of individual-versus-group payments to a "representative" body of black leaders, they will have to answer a host of prickly questions in selecting their decision-makers. Should the senate be composed solely of persons named by existing black organizations (churches, fraternal orders, reform groups, revolutionary committees, etc.), or should unaffiliated notables (e.g., poets, performers, intellectuals, and civil servants) also be included? In either case, *what* organizations and *what* individuals? Should those who are dissatisfied with, or apathetic to, all existing black organizations be represented? If the senate is to be representative, should the votes of its members be weighted, or should the principle be "one group, one vote"? Should the churches and fraternal orders be allowed to outvote the Black Panthers because of their large memberships, or are large numbers to be discounted on the theory that they reflect submission to or imitation of the white regime whose behavior is the very reason for demanding compensation? If the vanguard is to be allowed more votes than more slothful organizations, who is to decide whether a group that claims to be the vanguard is really only a body of stragglers because the army is moving in the opposite direction?

In short, any organization that wants advice on whether

reparations should be paid to individuals, groups, or both, must either select its advisers or promulgate the rules by which they are to be selected; and it must either prescribe the procedure by which the advisers shall act or promulgate the rules for determining how their procedure is to be determined. The advisers may reject these rules once they have convened, but unlike a revolutionary body that can seize power and supplant those who brought it into being, in the end they must present their recommendations (even if they are called non-negotiable demands) to the agency that convened them.

Nor can ultimate responsibility be avoided by substituting a popular plebiscite for a senate. For one thing, the decision to use a plebiscite instead of a senate—by hypothesis, a governmental choice—will itself influence the outcome; it requires no prescience to see that a popular vote is more likely to favor payments to individuals, while a senate would be predisposed to choose organizations as the ultimate recipients of the payments. Moreover, it would be argued that a plebiscite turns the fateful decision over to individuals who have been degraded and brainwashed, and that until their independence has been restored, their leaders—those who have thrown off the yoke—should be entrusted with authority.

Even if these objections to a plebiscite are rejected, the composition of the voting body would not be self-evident. If reparations are to be paid for such demonstrable effects of official racism as compulsory attendance at segregated schools, the qualifications of voters should be consistent with the right to participate in the distribution of benefits; but if the program is to compensate for a pervasive racism regardless of its impact on individuals, a larger group of voters would be appropriate. Since there are many possible circles of beneficiaries, there would be a corresponding diversity of potential voters. But this fact leads to the disturbing conclusion that the structure of the program may have to be designed before the plebiscite is held, thus undermining the hope for an "independent" black decision to be binding on the agency that is to make the payments.

Finally, whether a senate or a popular plebiscite is employed, there are no accepted rules to govern the degree of approval required to endorse one approach rather than another. One who starts with the assumption that individuals are entitled to reparations unless they agree voluntarily to assign their claims to a representative group of organizations would accept a program of group reparations only if it commanded a very high percentage of the votes in the hypothetical election. If the opposite assumption is the starting point, a similarly high vote might be demanded to validate individual payments, which would be seen as a proposal to divide the group's patrimony and thereby endanger its future as an entity. A suggestive analogy may be found in the painful problem of terminating federal supervision over Indian tribes —a step favored by some advocates of Indian self-determination because it would leave the Indians free to preserve their tribal organization, but opposed by others who argue that the prior dependency of tribal Indians has robbed many of them of the capacity to make "voluntary" decisions reflecting their "true" or "long-term" interests. Those who are critical of a plebiscite argue that the white man will be to blame if he allows tribal Indians to vote in favor of termination or to withdraw their ratable shares of tribal property and if disintegration follows.[85]

In my discussion so far, I have tacitly assumed that a program of black reparations, if adopted, would consist of payments in money. Although money was what James Forman demanded in Riverside Church, compensation could obviously take a variety of other forms. Section 1983 provides that liability to the injured party shall be established by "an action at law, suit in equity, or other proper proceeding for redress," and these separate procedural channels would lead to divergent solutions. Money damages are the normal outcome of "an action at law," but the remedial powers of a court of equity are more flexible and broad-ranging. In school desegregation cases, for example, Section 1983 has been used not merely to direct that improper practices be terminated, but also to require that detailed plans of compliance be formulated and presented for judicial approval. In some instances, the courts have themselves devised the plan, either by announcing the elements necessary for approval or by requiring the defendant school board to follow a pattern developed in another district. Among the components that the courts have either approved or insisted upon (as will be indicated in more detail in a later chapter) are provisions allowing black pupils to transfer to predominantly white schools, requiring racially mixed faculties, nullifying discriminatory tests for the appointment or promotion of schoolteachers and administrators, and the like.

Though the range of remedies open to the courts under Section 1983 is broad, a legislative body working in the same area has immeasurably greater discretion. A court can deal only with the parties before it and those "similarly situated," as defined by traditional concepts of judicial jurisdiction; the writs of a legislative body, by contrast, run throughout its kingdom. Moreover, the regulatory authority of the courts ordinarily embraces only those programs that the legislative and executive branches of government have chosen to put into force. Thus, Section 1983 does not require the states or municipalities to build libraries or swimming pools or public universities; its requirement of equality in administration arises, so to speak, only after these facilities have been created. In a few instances, to be sure, the courts have ordered the reopening of a public facility closed down by a local governmental body, but only when a discriminatory purpose and effect were manifest.[86] Save for such clumsy attempts to retaliate against blacks attempting to use a facility previously reserved for whites, a local refusal to appropriate money for a public program, no matter how customary or desirable, is not subject to judicial review under Section 1983.

Congress, however, need not confine itself to the elimination of discriminatory practices in existing programs and institutions. Unless the earmarking of benefits for a single racial group is forbidden by the Constitution (a subject to be discussed in a later chapter), Congress has virtually plenary power to establish a program of black reparations. Exercising its authority under the general-welfare and commerce clauses, augmented by its power under Section 5 of the Fourteenth Amendment to enforce the equal-protection clause, Congress could enact any legislation reasonably calculated to remedy the continuing effects of segregation and racial discrimination. The possibilities include the establishment of universities, training centers, and research institutes; the granting of preferences in civil service and private employment; and the prescription of differential pay scales.[87] But programs of this type, whether proposed as alternatives or supplements to compensatory payments in money, would not escape the problems to which this chapter has been devoted. They would, moreover, operate in a fragmentary manner, providing benefits for those blacks who fit within the prescribed categories or who desire to participate in the programs, while serving only a symbolic function for others. The greatest benefits might accrue to those who have been least disadvantaged by racial discrimination, as has been said of India's constitutional and statutory provisions—enacted on becoming independent of Great Britian—which reserved specified numbers of university places and government posts for the Scheduled Classes (i.e., the former Untouchables).[88]

In this chapter I have canvassed the problem of deciding between group and individual reparations not to imply that either type of program would be impractical, counterproductive, or impossible, but rather to dispel the illusion that its shape could be finally or authoritatively determined by the recipients so as to relieve the organization providing the funds from responsibility for these structural matters. Congress or some other public body, rather than its unofficial advisers, will have to decide in the end whether a program of reparations should consist of individual or group payments, specific nonmonetary programs, or some combination of these, and will have to face all the subordinate difficulties that each of these alternatives would bring in its wake.

9.

Compensation to Fit Each Beneficiary's Personal Circumstances?

If the beneficiaries of the reparations program are individuals rather than groups, should the same compensation be paid to everyone, or should the impact of racial discrimination upon each person be separately assessed in order to compensate him accordingly? Looking to Section 1983 for guidance, we find that it requires a separate inquiry into the damages suffered by each plaintiff. Averages, such as the comparative earning levels of blacks and whites of the same age or skill, might be used in assessing damages under Section 1983 but only as a rough pattern in tailoring the suit to fit the claimant. The ultimate objective is compensation commensurate with the damages suffered by the plaintiff himself. If this approach is employed in a comprehensive program of black reparations, we must face the consequences of making a separate calculation for each beneficiary. Along with the colossal task of assessing the evidence person-by-person for

millions of individuals (more easily handled by an administrative agency than by the courts), we must weigh the intra-
group competition that it would entail.

Compare, in this context, the circumstances of a Mississippi sharecropper, a Harlem welfare mother, a Fisk University professor, a successful jazz performer, an unemployed
young man living in a Chicago slum, a political leader in
Detroit, and a kindergarten child in a predominantly white
suburban school. Each would have to prove the amount of
his or her damages as an individual if the reparations program adopted the approach of Section 1983. If the income
gap between whites and blacks of equal potential is used to
measure damages, there would be one set of disparities in the
reparations owing to these persons; if we focus instead upon
the abrasive or humiliating experiences they have encountered, the compensation schedule would be quite different.
Should a black ghetto be regarded as a cocoon that insulates
its inhabitants from the difficulties that abound for the black
who lives and competes in a predominantly white environment, or is the isolation of the cocoon itself a source of
special injury? Do both of these life-styles—isolation and
integration—expose their members to more injury than is
suffered by the black who has "passed over" into the white
world without detection, or is he, to the contrary, worse off
because he must turn his back on relatives and old friends
lest he be unmasked? What of the black who has responded
to segregation by becoming a civil rights leader and who
might otherwise, like Vanzetti, have been only "a poor fish
peddler"; the "showcase" black in a white corporation whose
earnings are better than his white counterparts but who sus-
pects that he was chosen less for his personal merits than to
protect his employer against charges of discrimination; the
West Indian immigrant whose brighter occupational oppor-

tunities in the United States are marred by discrimination that he could have escaped by staying at home?

As these questions suggest, an attempt to individualize the compensation awarded in a program of black reparations would have to weigh so many imponderable elements of damage that despite the ideal of conformity to each claimant's personal circumstances, the recoveries might in the end be more capricious than accurate. This risk, coupled with the administrative cost of searching for a precision that is elusive at best, leads quite naturally to the consideration of an alternative measuring stick—a rough-and-ready rule of equality. As with the G.I. Bill of Rights and some other governmental programs, the core of such an alternative would be a schedule of benefits graduated by reference to a few readily ascertainable facts (such as the claimant's age and marital status) but otherwise disregarding his personal characteristics and life history.

Unfortunately, this response to the difficulties of individualizing the remedy generates its own problems. Difficult as it may be to draw distinctions among the victims of racial discrimination, it may be worse to ignore the differences. Just as the long-honored objective of equal opportunities for blacks and whites overlooks the obstacles facing the late entrant—the paradox of "equality in an unequal world"[89]— so a program of reparations treating all beneficiaries alike would be flawed because all beneficiaries are not alike. To return to the abbreviated case histories I offered earlier, even though all have experienced racial discrimination, it would be hard to justify—either to them or to others—identical treatment for a Harlem welfare mother and a Fisk University professor, or for an unemployed young resident of a Chicago slum and a Detroit political leader, unless the benefits of the program are trivial or merely symbolic. Whichever way the decision goes, it is bound to create powerful and justifiable grievances within the group that is intended to be compensated by the program.

The same may be said of the possible alternative or supplementary components of a black-reparations program, mentioned at the end of the previous chapter. A university, training center, or preferences in civil government employment, for example, would provide direct benefits to only a limited segment of the black population. Even more than a decision in favor of uniform rather than tailor-made compensation, the prospect of a reparations program with internally discriminatory components could stimulate a fratricidal struggle for primacy, whose outcome for the losers would be a deeper sense of injustice or betrayal. The moral achievement in acknowledging a duty to compensate for the past and in attempting to discharge this obligation may outweigh these dangers, but it is quixotic to think that black reparations will be less productive of painful side effects than other legislative responses to intractable social ailments.

10.

Identifying the Beneficiaries

A program to compensate children who were required to go to segregated schools before the Supreme Court's 1954 decision in *Brown v. Board of Education* would not raise any conceptual difficulties in identifying the beneficiaries. They would be the children who were enrolled in black schools in states with pre-1954 school-segregation laws. Just as a person who files a claim for social security or veterans' benefits must establish that he worked for the requisite period or served in the armed services, so a claimant under this hypothetical plan would have to establish that he attended a segregated school. Since benefits would be at stake, one would expect most of the program's intended beneficiaries to come forward with proof that they had been required to attend segregated schools. Their claims could be verified by school attendance records, and records that were lost or destroyed could be reconstructed by affidavits or other supporting evidence. The administrative job would, of course, be monumental, but the ultimate question to be decided would be simple: Was the claimant required to attend a segregated school by the local authorities?

If the compensation plan provided that benefits could be inherited by the children of a deceased student, the administrative job would be enlarged, but it would not be unprecedented: when a person entitled to social security or veterans' benefits dies, the administrative agencies must pass on disputed issues of kinship and inheritance in deciding who inherits his rights. Another parallel is the German compensation program for victims of Nazi prosecution, which manages to cope with claims by hundreds of thousands of refugees and their heirs, scattered from Hong Kong to Buenos Aires, whose only evidence of entitlement to reparations may be a letter from a person who died in a concentration camp, a notation in Gestapo records seized by an Allied military unit, or the fading recollection of an elderly neighbor of the claimant's parents.

Though a reparations program confined to students who were required by law to attend segregated schools would entail a large administrative job, it would not raise difficult or painful questions of racial classification. Entitlement would depend exclusively on the fact that the student was assigned to a black school, regardless of his actual racial origin. Thus, a student who was required by the state to attend a Negro school would be entitled to benefits whether or not he was properly classified as "Negro"; conversely, a Negro who covertly attended a white school would be excluded from benefits even though he would have been expelled if his racial make-up had been known to the authorities. Here again, I invoke by way of analogy the German compensation program, under which a person classified as a

Jew by the Nazi authorities is entitled to compensation even if the classification was erroneous under the rules then in force in Germany, and needless to say, even if he would not have been so classified under the standards in vogue elsewhere.

But if, to take account of a broader range of racial discrimination, the circle of persons entitled to reparations is enlarged beyond those who were required to attend segregated schools, we quickly encounter the conceptual issue that I have previously side-stepped, viz., Who is black? An authoritative answer to this question would be required, for example, if reparations were to be paid for the humiliation caused by the Jim Crow system. Since it would not be feasible to require proof from each person of whether and how often he was forced to use the segregated entrance to a public building, or the segregated part of a bus, theater, railroad waiting room, park, and so on, a comprehensive reparations program would perforce have to rely on a set of rules (possibly augmented by rebuttable presumptions) in defining the class of beneficiaries. One possibility would be to include only those who were immediately subject to a legally enforced system of segregation, such as blacks who lived in states with Jim Crow laws or who served in the armed forces before the end of World War II. In view of the national fall-out generated by the Jim Crow system, however, it would be more realistic to embrace all blacks throughout the country. In either variation, such a program of individual reparations would require an official answer to the question, Who is black?

Racial classification is not, of course, a new art. Though geneticists and anthropologists agree that there is no scientific way to classify individuals,[90] our society and others have long distinguished between whites and blacks. Moreover, the line has been drawn for legal purposes, not merely for such unofficial decisions as membership in social groups. For example, in reviewing the constitutional validity of a criminal conviction in American law, it is sometimes necessary to determine whether blacks were systematically excluded from jury service. Litigation in the school-desegregation area often requires federal courts to decide whether the racial make-up of a school is predominantly white or predominantly Negro. Similarly, government agencies and employers are sometimes asked for reports on the racial composition of their labor forces. These racial identifications, however, are made on a wholesale rather than retail basis and are customarily based on general impressions from looking at a sea of faces. Thus, federal agencies ordinarily employ a "visual census" to classify their employees for statistical purposes; if questionnaires are used, each respondent's self-identification is accepted automatically and without requiring that he swear to its accuracy.[91]

American law has also sometimes required the official determination of an individual's race, for example, in the enforcement of school segregation or anti-miscegenation laws. These laws are now defunct, but there are some circumstances in which evidence of an individual's race might still be required. Thus, for example, if a defendant in a criminal case is not entitled to object to the systematic exclusion of Negroes from the jury unless he is himself a Negro,[91a] his right to make the objection might depend on whether he is "really" black or only an impostor. In the absence of official genealogies or expert evidence of the individual's genetic composition, the resolution of disputed cases depends on reputation, the jury's visual impression, or the testimony of observers. For example:

> I have seen Mr. McGhee, and he appears to have colored features. They are more darker than mine. I haven't got near enough to the man to recognize his eyes. I have seen Mrs. McGhee, and she appears to be the mulatto type.[92]

A racial test based on self-designation and reputation was evidently endorsed by a federal court in a recent desegregation case, when a Florida school board, in an obvious attempt to avoid compliance with a judicial decree, reported that it did not know how to classify its teachers and students by race, and then reported that they were all "Orientals." The court held, in this context, that a school board that had been able in the past to identify Negroes in order to segregate them should be able to identify them "with similar ease" in desegregating the school system. It also quoted, with apparent approval, the Department of Health, Education and Welfare's definition of Negroes, viz., "persons considered by themselves, by the school or by the community to be of African or Negro origin."[92a]

A large-scale program of black reparations, however, could not be administered without a more formal set of eligibility rules. It would hardly be fair or constitutionally permissible to grant benefits if in the judgment of the administrator, a court, or a body of laymen the applicant "appears to have colored features," and to deny them if his appearance fails to meet this standard. There has been enough mating across racial lines in the United States to justify the prediction that hundreds of thousands, if not millions, of persons of debatable racial composition might apply for compensation if the benefits were worth pursuing. It has been estimated that over thirty-six million Americans classified as white in 1960 had "an African element in their inherited biological background."[93] This means that the Africans brought to the United States have more "white" than "black" descendants.

It would be tempting to experiment with self-certification, allowing anyone identifying himself as black to receive reparations if he is willing to accept the public consequences of that classification. Recent experience with political pranksters, however, suggests that persons opposed to black reparations would not hesitate to file claims for benefits, knowing that whites masquerading as blacks for this purpose would not have to pay the price that society has imposed on genuine blacks; and these Abbie Hoffmans of the racial right might even win the admiration of their neighbors for outwitting or discrediting "the system." False claims might also be filed by persons with grievances, real or imagined, that in their own opinions entitle them to the status of "white niggers." These claims could not be denied, nor could the claimants be punished, without an officially sanctioned mode of proving that the applicant was not black.[94] A useful analogy is the administration of the federal income tax, which commences with the taxpayer's own statement of his income and deductions. The return is provisionally accepted as accurate, but when it is audited by the Internal Revenue Service, the taxpayer has the burden of proving the propriety of all challenged entries. If a reparations program allowed the claimant to make a similar initial certification of his rights, the procedure could be protected against abuse only by penalizing false claims, and this safeguard would require an official code of racial classification to separate the sheep from the goats.

For guidance in this seemingly indispensable process of racial classification, the laws used by the Southern states to enforce their segregation and anti-miscegenation laws could be resurrected; or, because these definitions conflicted with each other and were far from uniform, a panel of legal experts could be assembled and charged with the duty of extracting the "best" (or would it be the "worst"?) rule from this medley—the essence of racism, so to speak. If these sources are too provincial or antiquated for the modern temper, we could turn to the preeminent contemporary fountainhead: South Africa, whose scholars—heirs to both English and Roman-Dutch legal traditions—have explored every facet of this subject. Their work culminated in the enactment in 1950 of the Population Registration Act, under which every person's racial classification is recorded in a kind of Doomsday Book; unless successfully appealed to the courts, this classification is final and binding.[95]

I venture to predict that the adoption of a formal code of racial classification, whether home-grown or imported, would have calamitous consequences for the United States. It would ease the way to more and more private, public, and official distinctions between black and white. It would put pressure on millions of persons of mixed blood to make an official declaration of their racial origin, instead of allowing their allegiance to remain private, ambiguous, submerged, neglected, or changeable. To be sure, they could protect their privacy by forgoing their benefits, but for many this would be an intolerable price. Some black nationalists might welcome official support for the process of racial identification, as would some white groups; but surely the legitimate objectives of groups seeking greater awareness of black history and a more intense racial pride can be served by the voluntary adherence of the persons to whom their messages are addressed. While the government should not build obstacles to the achievement of these objectives, it should be equally careful not to act as a recruiting office.

It may be said in response that we are already two societies, black and white, and that official racial classifications would do no more than accept the universe. But the theory that we are already so divided that no official action could increase the separation is as fatuous as the theory—so prevalent on college campuses in the spring of 1970—that official repression was already so total that no amount of reactionary backlash could make matters worse. In a dynamic world, governmental intervention is bound to push us one way or the other. The proposed code is more likely to reinforce and sharpen polarization than to reduce racial separation.

There is undoubtedly a bitter irony in arguing that a country that used racial classifications for many years should be wary of preserving or reviving them in a program of reparations. As pointed out earlier, however, it is one thing to permit persons who were required to attend segregated schools to recover damages under a corrective statute, such as Section 1983, which (like the German reparations program) simply accepts the past racial classification, whether "valid" or not, as a basis for corrective action. It is something else again to establish a bureaucratic apparatus to determine the race of persons who were never officially classified for such purposes as school segregation, especially since those who do not wish to submit to this process will have to sacrifice a financial benefit in order to preserve their privacy. Quite aside from persons of debatable racial ancestry who prefer ambiguity to clarification, there are surely many persons of undeniable black descent who will resent an official code of racial classification even though they acknowledge without cavil or proudly proclaim their *négritude*. The problems discussed here, to be sure, already exist in embryo in a variety of programs undertaken in recent years to counteract the effects of racial segregation and discrimination. School-desegregation plans, for example, sometimes permit a child who belongs to a racial majority in his school to transfer to a school where he will be in the minority; and preferential employment and college-admissions plans may on occasion require a person of disputed racial ancestry to prove his classification.[96] Given the fragmentary and experimental nature of these arrangements, it may be possible to administer them without elaborate administrative devices to resolve debatable racial claims; but they are hardly persuasive precedents for a comprehensive program of black reparations.

In addition to the dangers just canvassed, a code of racial classification could lead to a Balkanization of the racial map. South Africa, for example, uses the classifications "European," "Bantu," and "Coloured," the latter group being subdivided into "Cape Coloured," "Indian," "Malay," and four other categories. Similarly, in responding to claims by American Indians, we have indulged in some fine distinctions. For example, a recent Senate-approved bill relating to Alaskan natives provided that a person of one-quarter or more Indian, Eskimo, or Aleut blood would qualify for benefits, but that Tsimshian Indian blood would not count, nor the blood of any other Indian tribe that migrated to Alaska after 1867; and there is other legislation in force that distinguishes between "full blood" and "mixed blood" Indians.[97] Rules of this type may be unavoidable in dealing with Indian tribes, since the very concept of a tribe implies a connection by blood among its members, but the extension of the process to other social groupings should not be undertaken lightly. The burgeoning of "ethnic studies" in schools and colleges suggests some of the possibilities in the official classification of individuals, initially in the compilation of statistics and then in the administration of remedial programs for their benefit. The process would be complicated still further by the ambiguity of the term "ethnic," currently often used to denote groups characterized by national or regional origin, language, religion, or other traits, regardless of racial ancestry.

Even if confined to blacks, a racial code would invite distinctions—already familiar in American law[98]—based on the individual's percentage of "African blood." This would, indeed, not be irrational in a system of black reparations, since the impact of discrimination depends in part on the degree to which a person is perceived as black by society, as well as on his self-perception. If a program of black reparations were to take account of these differences, however, it would ineluctably pit one subgroup against another in the race for benefits: should a mulatto get one-half the benefit of a full-blooded black, a quadroon one-quarter, etc.?

At first glance, it might be thought that these problems would afflict only a program of individual reparations and could be avoided by shifting to group reparations. On examination, however, this strategy—which might be rejected for the reasons canvassed in Chapter 8 ("Compensation to Groups or to Individuals?") even if it promised sure deliverance from the perils of a racial code—proves to be unequal to the task, except at the cost of additional difficulties. The simplest case is a program confined to groups with black constituencies of their own, such as black universities and economic-development corporations. Since the legitimacy of their participation would depend upon the racial composition of their respective clienteles, these organizations would have to promulgate and apply their own racial codes to establish and preserve their credentials. As conduits for the flow of governmental benefits to their constituencies, however, they would at most disguise, without diluting, public responsibility for their racial policies. Nor could Congress, if it empowered such an organization to administer a publicly financed program, wash its hands of the procedures used by its instrumentality to decide individual cases of disputed entitlement to participate in the benefits.

Thus, Indian tribes, despite their long-acknowledged "internal sovereignty,"[99] were subjected by the Civil Rights Act of 1964 to most of the constitutional restraints imposed on the federal and state governments by the first fourteen amendments. Had Congress not explicitly imposed these limitations on tribal self-government, it is quite possible that the federal courts would have moved in this direction on their own. The recent judicial tendency to require a wide variety of "private" organizations to conform to such constitutional concepts as "due process" and "equal protection" could hardly have been expected to take a detour around every Indian reservation in the country.[100] The pressure would be even greater to impose similar requirements, by either legislative or judicial action, on organizations that lack the Indian tribe's historic and treaty-protected right to internal sovereignty. The organization's decisions to grant or deny government-financed benefits would surely rank high on any list of matters which could not be allowed to escape official scrutiny and revision.

The need for a racial code would dwindle, and its role would become less obtrusive, if the hypothetical program of group reparations embraced "black-managed" organizations, regardless of the racial composition of their audiences (e.g., newspapers, radio and television stations, museums and galleries, training centers, and universities with racially mixed student bodies). A familiar American pattern is the voluntary agency that preserves a religious tinge at the trusteeship level while providing services without regard to the religious affiliation of the consumers, e.g., the Y.M.C.A., Notre Dame University, and Mount Sinai Hospital. However, if the group recipients of black reparations followed a

similar open-door policy, the racial content of their programs would soon be only a symbolic vestige, or a vestigial
symbol, of their history. Lovers of African music, soul food,
and LeRoi Jones' plays would go to the Malcolm X Cultural
Center, for example, in the same way that people who want
to swim, lose weight, or learn karate go to the Y.M.C.A.—
without reference to their own religious affiliations and with
equal disregard for the organization's historic roots. As an
instrument of reparations, the organization would in time be
no more distinctive than a national park, historic site, or
museum of Negro history.

While reducing the need for a racial code, such a program
of group reparations would require a host of ultimately arbitrary choices among the organizations that would clamor for
participation. For example: should proof of a predominantly
black constituency entitle an organization to receive benefits,
regardless of its objectives? To illustrate the potential for
conflict, assume that applications are filed by four organizations concerned with the geographical location of blacks,
favoring (a) a back-to-Africa movement, (b) independent
black nationhood for a group of American states, (c) emigra-
tion from inner cities to suburban areas, and (d) concentration in the inner city. If each group claims a monopoly on
wisdom, asserting that its competitors are dominated by ti-
midity, ignorance, servility, romanticism, or selfishness,
should the merits of each program be assessed, or should all
four be regarded as equally deserving of assistance? In granting tax exemptions to nonprofit organizations, ideology ordinarily does not count; at the organizational level, this form
of neutrality means that the group can keep whatever it can
raise from its members and admirers without being burdened
by taxes. In theory, this approach could be employed in
dispensing reparations by matching any contributions that

the organization can attract from private sources (dollar for dollar or according to a more complex formula). Once begun, this procedure would be as self-executing as tax exemptions; but it would probably not command the support needed to reach the launching pad. This is because the largest black voluntary agencies are churches, fraternal lodges, and the NAACP; in this context, a reparations program consisting of matching grants would be hopelessly lopsided. Another source of difficulty is inherent in the vague concept of "black control." If this, rather than the racial composition of an organization's membership or clientele, is to determine the group's right to receive reparations, must its officers, directors, or staff be exclusively, predominantly, or significantly black? Would the Urban League, with its biracial board of directors, qualify; or Hampton University, with its biracial board and a growing percentage of white students; or the black studies program of Cornell University; or the black apprenticeship program of the United Automobile Workers?

The friction that would be caused by governmental answers to these and similar questions might be mollified by entrusting the decisions to a board of black representatives. To get this insulation, however, the government would first have to select these black notables, and unless they were constituted as a self-perpetuating body, it would have to pick their successors as well. As argued in Chapter 8 ("Compensation to Groups or to Individuals?"), this process would simultaneously proclaim that an aggregation of diverse individuals makes up a homogeneous collectivity, stir up justified resentment among those who were not selected for official recognition, and expose those who were selected to the charge of being official spokesmen despite their alleged representative character.

In conclusion, my inquiry into the problem of identifying the beneficiaries of a program of black reparations drives me to make two equally bleak observations: that compensation to individuals could not be administered without a racial code and a large-scale procedure for the racial classification of individuals; and that group reparations would mitigate or eliminate this hazard only to embrace the equally grave hazards of selecting, with no satisfactory guideposts, the black organizations to participate in the program or creating an official body of black "representatives" to make these decisions. It is the justice of reparations when viewed in the large, coupled with these perils of administering a program in the concrete, that lead me to perceive this area as the locus of a second American Dilemma.

11.

The Constitutionality of Black Reparations

Does the Constitution permit the federal government to establish and finance a program of reparations whose benefits would go to black citizens exclusively? It is, of course, common practice for governmental benefits to be distributed to a limited class of persons. Thus, we take it for granted that poor people but not rich ones get welfare payments, that veterans but not non-veterans qualify for benefits under the G.I. Bill of Rights, that homeowners but not tenants qualify for home-mortgage guarantees, and that farmers but not city people qualify for farm price supports and agricultural extension services. Moreover, in an earlier age the lines of demarcation drawn by Congress or the state legislature in the distribution of benefits were virtually immune to judicial review; echoing the popular maxim that beggars can't be choosers, it was said that no one has a constitutional right to public "largesse." This curt response is no longer in vogue,

and the courts are now more willing to review the qualifications laid down in legislation on the complaint of an ag-
grieved person to see if his exclusion is so unreasonable as to
violate the Fifth Amendment's guarantee of "due process of
law" or the Fourteenth Amendment's guarantee of "equal
protection of the laws."[101] In these judicial forays, however,
the courts acknowledge that legislative bodies have an ex-
ceedingly wide range for the exercise of discretion, and the
legislative judgment is rarely overturned.

Against this background, black reparations might be regarded as simply a routine legislative action to meet the
claims of one defined group of citizens by establishing a
program from which others (viz., whites) are excluded.
Asked to enlarge the program to include whites (for example,
on the ground that many whites have also suffered from
governmental neglect or misconduct), or to enjoin its operation entirely, the Supreme Court might repeat what it said
when an Oklahoma optician argued that he was denied the
equal protection of the laws by a state law that regulated his
business but exempted the sellers of ready-to-wear eyeglasses
with which his products competed:

> The problem of legislative classification is a perennial one, ad-
> mitting of no doctrinaire definition. Evils in the same field may
> be of different dimensions and proportions, requiring different
> remedies. Or so the legislature may think. Or the reform may
> take one step at a time, addressing itself to the phase of the
> problem which seems most acute to the legislative mind. The
> legislature may select one phase of one field and apply a remedy
> there, neglecting the others. The prohibition of the Equal Protec-
> tion Clause goes no further than the invidious discrimination.[102]

In a similar vein, the Supreme Court upheld the conviction
of a Maryland storekeeper for selling a loose-leaf binder and

a can of floor wax in violation of the state's Sunday closing laws, despite the fact that the laws exempted the sale of cigarettes, gasoline, candy, and a bewildering array of other products. Rejecting the defendant's argument that these statutory distinctions were so arbitrary and capricious as to deny him the equal protection of the laws, the Court said:

> Although no precise formula has been developed, the Court has held that [the equal-protection clause of] the Fourteenth Amendment permits the States a wide scope of discretion in enacting laws which affect some groups of citizens differently than others. The constitutional safeguard is offended only if the classification rests on grounds wholly irrelevant to the achievement of the State's objective. State legislatures are presumed to have acted within their constitutional power despite the fact that, in practice, their laws result in some inequality. A statutory discrimination will not be set aside if any state of facts reasonably may be conceived to justify it.[103]

Although expressed in cases involving the constitutionality of state action under the equal-protection clause, judicial deference to the legislature's judgment is an equally common response when federal action is attacked under the due-process clause of the Fifth Amendment.

This reluctance to interfere with legislative solutions, however, does not extend to laws embodying distinctions based on race, color, or religion. They encounter a more skeptical reception, epitomized in the Supreme Court's statement that

> Distinctions between citizens solely because of their ancestry are by their very nature odious to a free people whose institutions are founded upon the doctrine of equality.[104]

More succinctly, Justice Harlan said in 1896 that the "Constitution is color-blind." He made this remark in his dissenting opinion in *Plessy v. Ferguson,* where the majority upheld a state segregation statute; but it is often said that his view was vindicated and endorsed by *Brown v. Board of Education* in 1954, when the Supreme Court overruled the *Plessy* case.

Can these generalizations, founded on the equal-protection clause of the Fourteenth Amendment and also on a more basic theory of democracy, be squared with racial distinctions having a compensatory purpose? Or do they confine governmental actions to the elimination of racial disparities for the future, requiring us to let bygones be bygones? It is interesting to discover that Section 5 of the Fourteenth Amendment, authorizing Congress to enact appropriate legislation to enforce the amendment's prohibitions, was once described by the Supreme Court as having an exclusively racial purpose. "We doubt very much," said the Court in 1872, "whether any action of a State not directed by way of discrimination against the negroes as a class, or on account of their race, will ever be held to come within the purview of this provision."[105] This prophecy was not borne out, however, and commentators in recent years have often asserted that legislation for the exclusive benefit of one racial group would violate the Fourteenth Amendment even if animated by a remedial or benign purpose.[106] Section 1983 does not raise such doubts, although the legislative history related in Chapter 3 shows that its beneficiaries were expected to be black victims of the Ku Klux Klan, because it does not single out blacks as such, but provides in general terms for compensation to anyone whose constitutional rights have been violated under color of state law. But the validity of a reparations program exclusively for blacks is less clear, especially if equal benefits are to be paid regardless of the varying impact of segregation and other forms of official discrimination on the individual claimant.

Ten years ago I struggled with these issues in an article entitled "The Case of the Checker-Board Ordinance: An Experiment in Race Relations."[107] My arena was an imaginary lawsuit brought by a Negro who had been denied the right to buy a house designated for "white occupancy only" in New Harmony, Illinois, a utopian community in which every dwelling was assigned to either black or white occupancy in a checkerboard pattern. In my fable the ordinance was enacted to achieve integration by legal compulsion, following testimony by students of American race relations that private discrimination and prejudice are heightened by segregated, and lowered by integrated, housing patterns; that a community with a stable pattern of integrated housing would enrich the lives of all its citizens by enlarging their relations with persons of the other race; and that whites either would not move to New Harmony or would tend to leave if they thought they would be greatly outnumbered by Negroes. The central issue in this hypothetical lawsuit was whether the equal-protection clause of the Fourteenth Amendment permits citizens to be classified by race in the administration of a "benign" governmental program.

Because I found the question troublesome and resistant to a clear solution, I cast the discussion in the form of separate opinions by three appellate judges. The first judge wrote the briefest opinion, concluding that the Constitution prohibits the use of race or color as a criterion of state action, at least in regulating the ownership and occupancy of land. He relied primarily on two Supreme Court decisions. One, decided in 1917, held that a municipal ordinance forbidding blacks to move into or occupy houses in residential blocks that were predominantly occupied by whites (and imposing reciprocal restrictions on whites) violated the due-process clause of the

Fourteenth Amendment.[108] The other, announced in 1948, cited the equal-protection clause in holding that state courts could not enforce restrictive covenants voluntarily adopted by private landowners to preserve the racial character of their neighborhoods, even though the state courts stood ready to enforce such covenants against potential white occupants as well as against blacks:

> The rights established [by the Fourteenth Amendment] are personal rights. . . . Equal protection of the laws is not achieved through indiscriminate imposition of inequalities.[109]

My hypothetical judge's conclusion that New Harmony's checkerboard ordinance was inconsistent with these cases was reinforced, in his opinion, by the Supreme Court's 1954 condemnation of public school segregation in *Brown v. Board of Education.*

For my second hypothetical judge, this conclusion was an unacceptable interpretation of the Constitution. He accused his colleague of mechanically applying constitutional provisions designed to prevent discrimination against the newly emancipated slaves to a very different area, viz., remedial or compensatory legislation:

> The Fourteenth Amendment is almost one hundred years old, and its life has been replete with irony: railroads, utility companies, banks, employers of child labor, chain stores, money lenders, aliens, and a host of other groups and institutions have all found nurture in the due process and equal protection clauses, leaving so little room for the Negro that he seemed to be the fourteenth amendment's forgotten man. This despite the Supreme Court's early recognition that "the one pervading purpose" of the thirteenth, fourteenth, and fifteenth amendments was to insure "the freedom of the slave race, the security and firm establishment of that freedom, and the protection of the

newly-made freeman and citizen from the oppressions of those who had formerly exercised unlimited dominion over him" . . . . The kaleidoscope of life often refuses to reflect our confident predictions, but seldom has a forecast been so completely lost to sight. Even so, the crowning irony comes today, when the racial zoning, restrictive covenant and school segregation cases, which had begun to restore the fourteenth amendment to the Negro, are used as weapons to destroy the first local legislation to ameliorate the condition of the Negro that has passed in review before this court.

In harmony with this approach, my second judge distinguished the cases on which the first judge had relied, arguing that racial classifications are not unconstitutional per se, but only if they impute inferiority to one of the groups:

> Any legislation that treats individuals (minors, women, men of draft age, veterans, lawyers, Indians, etc.) as members of a class necessarily distinguishes them from others; but the legislation does not "discriminate" (in an invidious sense) if the classification is validated by some appropriate purpose or effect.

To illustrate this principle, the second judge pointed out that race has often been used by the courts as a factor in passing on the constitutionality of criminal convictions:

> In reviewing criminal cases in which violations of the due process clause have been alleged (e.g., denial of counsel, involuntary confessions, unreasonable delays in arraignment, etc.) the federal courts have often referred to the defendant's race or color. Without suggesting that race or color were crucial in all of these cases, or indeed in any, I cannot believe that they were merely neutral circumstances, like the defendant's social security number. Race, to the contrary, has been treated as a relevant circumstance, like the defendant's youth, poverty, illiteracy, or friendlessness, in judging whether he received due process of law. Rigorous proof of racial prejudice has not been demanded,

however, and it would not be unreasonable to describe these cases as exercises of benevolent vigilance thought necessary to protect Negroes as a class from improper practices by the police and trial courts.

Other racial classifications that are permitted because of their "remedial" character, according to my second judge, are the restricted rights of certain American Indians to dispose of their property until the Secretary of the Interior certified them as competent to handle their own affairs, and cases permitting a black defendant in a criminal case to get a new trial if blacks were systematically excluded from his jury. He went on to conclude that the checkerboard ordinance, though it restricted the freedom of the Negro plaintiff to live where he wished, was a similarly reasonable effort to correct a social evil, and that it was consistent with the constitutional guarantees of due process and equal protection.

The third judge argued that this distinction between benign and malevolent uses of racial classifications threatened to undermine the constitutional objective of equality. If a checkerboard pattern of individual houses is permissible, why not a checkerboard of city blocks or wards, or a local white–black ratio corresponding to the state or national ratio or to a sociologist's recipe for a "good mix" of racial groups? If housing is a permissible area for experimentation, why not proportional racial representation in schools, employment, or voting? If these quotas, limitations, and privileges are permissible ways to compensate for past injustices toward blacks, why not similar devices for other minorities, distinguished by religion, national origin, or economic status? At a more fundamental level, the third judge rejected his colleague's theory that benign racial legislation can be distinguished from legislation that imputes inferiority to one of the groups:

> Even the most well-intended legislation may be felt as humiliating by its objects, and especially so in a country that professes that "all men are created equal". . . .
>
> Viewed in this light, [New Harmony's] ordinance carries with it the offensive implication that is the unfortunate but seemingly inevitable concomitant of official charity or paternalism. Beyond that, it rests on, or is tantamount to, an official finding that whites will not live side-by-side with Negroes except under legal compulsion. Perhaps this will be regarded by some as an official condemnation of the attitude of whites, in no sense reflecting adversely on Negroes; but just as many Negroes could not write off racial segregation in the public schools as merely a monument to white inhumanity, so I doubt if the implications of the New Harmony's ordinance will leave them unscathed. Rather, many Negroes may ask themselves, as victims of private prejudice often do, what they have done to instill such distaste in others; and this inward search—made more acute by the fact that similar legal measures are not deemed necessary for other minority groups—may be equally destructive of self-esteem whether the finding that integrated housing cannot be achieved without legal compulsion is correct or not.

As to the Indian cases cited by his colleague to establish that the Constitution permits racial classifications of a remedial character, my third judge argued that they should serve instead "to warn us that the role of the Great White Father may be bitterly resented by those in his tutelage and that a guardian ordinarily prefers to postpone rather than to advance the day when his wards must face the rigors of freedom." He went on to say that even if the criminal cases involving black defendants, on which his colleague relied, display a rule of "benevolent vigilance" for the rights of blacks, this does not "lead to the conclusion that legislatures may exercise in other areas of life whatever benevolent supervision they may believe is required by the social problems they perceive."

In 1962, when I took both sides in this inconclusive debate, the constitutionality of "remedial" racial classifications was only a cloud on the distant horizon. It was perceived as a problem primarily by a few public housing agencies that were covertly applying a "benign" quota on black occupancy to prevent it from reaching the "tipping point" at which whites were expected to move out. Since then, however, the cloud has appeared directly overhead, blown here by the winds of change let loose by *Brown v. Board of Education,* and it threatens to deluge us with problems.

When *Brown* was decided, it was widely thought that compliance with its mandate "to admit [schoolchildren] to public schools on a racially nondiscriminatory basis" could be achieved by the repeal of all school segregation laws and the assignment of pupils to schools on the basis of school districts with "neutral" boundaries (e.g., highways, rivers, railroad tracks, and political subdivisions). Thus, the brief for the plaintiffs in *Brown* described the basic question in the case as "[w]hether the State of Kansas has power to enforce a state statute pursuant to which racially segregated public elementary schools are maintained." This suggested that the existence of predominantly or wholly black or white schools would not violate the Constitution, provided the new school-attendance zones followed "neutral" boundaries and were not gerrymandered in order to perpetuate a division along racial lines. The goal of *Brown v. Board of Education,* it was argued by the proponents of this limited mode of compliance, was not integration but the elimination of compulsory segregation. Indeed, some argued that the deliberate selection of boundaries to achieve a "desirable" racial mix would be improper, basing this conclusion on the theory of a color-blind Constitution.

In the intervening years these limited views of the requirements of *Brown* have been confronted by a very different approach, which insists on an actually integrated racial mix, even if it can be achieved only by racially determined school assignments or zones. The change is partly attributable to a growing recognition that today's housing patterns do not reflect unalloyed "voluntary" choice, but have been influenced by a host of governmental policies, including the school segregation laws themselves, the location and rental programs of public housing projects and other government-financed buildings, the judicial enforcement of private racially restrictive covenants in prior years, and the mortgage practices of public and government-financed private agencies. Thus, school attendance zones coinciding with a racial housing pattern that is itself based on official, even if unwritten, assumptions about the Negro's "proper" geographical place in the community have come to be viewed with skepticism. Moreover, in most if not all communities, there is a wide choice of ostensibly nonracial boundaries for attendance zones. If the use of First Avenue as a boundary serves to concentrate blacks in one school and whites in another, whereas Second Avenue would have produced integrated schools, it may be hard to overcome the suspicion that racial rather than traffic patterns dictated the choice. Rivers, railroad tracks, and interstate highways are less vulnerable to criticism, but even these dividers are rarely insuperable obstacles to the safe movement of schoolchildren in a mobile society.

Rather than indulge the presumption that the school board has acted in good faith, courts and administrative agencies with review responsibility for desegregation plans may demand evidence that the choice among equally plausible boundaries was not racially motivated, imposing either a light or a heavy burden of proof on this issue. A more stringent approach, reflecting either a disinclination to probe the mental processes of public officials or a more general view that "the Devil himself knoweth not the mind of man," is to examine a variety of possible boundaries, possibly with the aid of outside experts on school administration, and to require adoption of those most apt to produce integrated schools.

As courts and administrative agencies have turned from the mere nullification of formal segregation laws to the close scrutiny of ostensibly neutral school attendance boundaries, the actual racial composition of public schools has become a routine subject of discussion in judicial opinions. Moreover, the use of racial percentages as "ideals," "guides," and "points of departure" in the discussion of pupil-assignment plans has become equally routine. Similar references to racial percentages are common in the judicial review of school-board practices in locating and constructing new schools, closing old ones, choosing between consolidated and neighborhood schools, hiring, promoting, assigning, and firing teachers and principals, and prescribing curricula. This everyday use of racial statistics seems to reject Justice Harlan's concept of a "color-blind Constitution" which "does not . . . permit any public authority to know the race of those entitled to be protected in the enjoyment of [civil] rights."[110]

The propriety of racial distinctions and percentages in governmental action came to the fore in a recent Supreme Court decision, *Swann v. Charlotte-Mecklenburg Board of Education,* involving the busing of black children to predominantly white schools, and vice versa, under a desegregation plan designed by a court-appointed expert for a countywide school district that had formerly maintained a dual school system of the classic variety.[111] Under the heading "Remedial Altering of Attendance Zones," the Supreme Court described the plan, and endorsed it in sweeping terms:

> The maps submitted in these cases graphically demonstrate that one of the principal tools employed by school planners and by courts to break up the dual school system has been a frank —and sometimes drastic—gerrymandering of school districts and attendance zones. An additional step was pairing, "clustering," or "grouping" of schools with attendance assignments made deliberately to accomplish the transfer [by bus] of Negro students out of formerly segregated Negro schools and transfer of white students to formerly all-Negro schools. More often than not, these zones are neither compact nor contiguous; indeed they may be on opposite ends of the city. As an interim corrective measure, this cannot be said to be beyond the broad remedial powers of a court.
>
> Absent a constitutional violation there would be no basis for judicially ordering assignment of students on a racial basis. All things being equal, with no history of discrimination, it might well be desirable to assign pupils to schools nearest their homes. But all things are not equal in a system that has been deliberately constructed and maintained to enforce racial segregation. The remedy for such segregation may be administratively awkward, inconvenient and even bizarre in some situations and may impose burdens on some; but all awkwardness and inconvenience cannot be avoided in the interim period when remedial adjustments are being made to eliminate the dual school systems.

The Court, however, seemed to be more comfortable with the results of the plan than with the principles that underlay it, which, as described by the District Court, were:

that efforts should be made to reach a 71–29 ratio [of white to black pupils] in the various schools so that there will be no basis for contending that one school is racially different from the others . . ., that no school [should] be operated with an all-black or predominantly black student body, [and] that pupils of all grades [should] be assigned in such a way that as nearly as practicable the various schools at various grade levels have about the same proportion of black and white students.

The Supreme Court said of these racial percentages that a court could not properly require "any particular degree of racial balance or mixing" in a school desegregation plan, but that mathematical ratios could be used as "a starting point in the process of shaping a remedy." Finding that the plan under review did not embody an inflexible requirement of racial integration, the Court upheld the district court's order:

> [A] school authority's remedial plan or a district court's remedial decree is to be judged by its effectiveness. Awareness of the racial composition of the whole school system is likely to be a useful starting point in shaping a remedy to correct past constitutional violations. In sum, the very limited use made of mathematical ratios was within the equitable remedial discretion of the District Court.

But once a racial percentage is adopted as a starting point, any factors favoring its modification or abandonment may be rejected as unpersuasive, with the result that the school board will remain where it starts. After all, in using the term "starting point," the Court does not mean that the ultimate objective is to get some distance away, as is true of the "starting point" for a 100-yard dash. Thus, a racial quota employed as an interim measure (e.g., the "initial ratio" of at least two black teachers out of every twelve in each school, fixed in a case[112] that foreshadowed the result in the *Char-*

lotte-Mecklenburg case) may turn out to be very long-lived, notwithstanding the court's retained power to modify the quota or repeal it as conditions change. Longevity may also be the fate of a provision allowing students in a racial majority in their assigned schools to transfer to a school where they will be in a minority, described in *Charlotte-Mecklenburg* as "an indispensable remedy for those students willing to transfer to other schools in order to lessen the impact on them of the state-imposed stigma of segregation," and thus by inference regarded as a privilege created for black students.

The Supreme Court has not only upheld the discretionary use of racial percentages by school boards in dismantling a dual system, but has gone on to hold that they cannot be denied the use of this tool. The occasion for holding that racial percentages are a constitutionally protected device was a case involving a North Carolina statute, enacted in 1969, providing that "[n]o student shall be assigned or compelled to attend any school on account of race, creed, color or national origin, or for the purpose of creating a balance or ratio of race, religion, or national origins." Although this statute would have been a smashing victory for civil rights in 1900 or even 1950, the Court held in 1971 that it was unconstitutional:

> The legislation before us flatly forbids assignment of any student on account of race or for the purpose of creating a racial balance or ratio in the schools. The prohibition is absolute, and it would inescapably operate to obstruct the remedies granted by the District Court [in Swann v. Charlotte-Mecklenburg Board of Education]. But more important, the statute exploits an apparently neutral form to control school assignment plans by directing that they be "color blind"; that requirement, against the background of segregation, would render illusory

the promise of Brown v. Board of Education, 347 U.S. 483
(1954). Just as the race of students must be considered in determining whether a constitutional violation has occurred, so also
must race be considered in formulating a remedy. To forbid, at
this stage, all assignments made on the basis of race would
deprive school authorities of the one tool absolutely essential to
fulfillment of their constitutional obligation to eliminate existing
dual school systems.

Similarly the flat prohibition against assignment of students
for the purpose of creating a racial balance must inevitably
conflict with the duty of school authorities to disestablish dual
school systems. As we have held in *Swann*, the Constitution
does not compel any particular degree of racial balance or mixing, but when past and continuing constitutional violations are
found, some ratios are likely to be useful starting points in
shaping a remedy. An absolute prohibition against use of such
a device—even as a starting point—contravenes the implicit
command of Green v. County School Board, 391 U.S. 430 (1968),
that all reasonable methods be available to formulate an effective remedy.[113]

This burgeoning of racial quotas and percentages in the
school desegregation area seems to imply that we can have
a color-blind society in the long run only if we refuse to be
color-blind in the short run. The remedy, in short, is some
hair of the dog that bit us.

I have reviewed these developments in the school desegregation and related areas because of their bearing on the use
of "remedial" racial classifications in a program of black
reparations. They display a tolerance toward racial distinctions, when actively employed to dismantle dual school systems, that was anticipated by few if any commentators when
Brown v. Board of Education was decided. Whether born of
wisdom or despair, this tolerance can hardly be confined to
school desegregation plans. Dual schools having been only

one manifestation of the Jim Crow system, efforts to eradicate its consequences in such other areas as public employment, housing, voting registration, municipal services, and places of public accommodation will probably be permitted to employ equal weapons. Indeed, racial percentages are already familiar in programs to wipe out discrimination in employment, union membership, and college admissions, although in these areas they have not yet received the imprimatur of the Supreme Court.[114]

Recent school desegregation cases offer a second source of constitutional support for the racial restrictions inherent in black reparations by acknowledging that school boards have more discretion than the courts in relating educational programs to the needs of society. This point was explicitly made by the Supreme Court in the *Charlotte-Mecklenburg* case:

> Remedial judicial authority does not put judges automatically in the shoes of school authorities whose powers are plenary. Judicial authority enters only when local authority defaults.
>
> School authorities are traditionally charged with broad power to formulate and implement educational policy and might well conclude, for example, that in order to prepare students to live in a pluralistic society each school should have a prescribed ratio of Negro to white students reflecting the proportion for the district as a whole. To do this as an educational policy is within the broad discretionary powers of school authorities; absent a finding of a constitutional violation, however, that would not be within the authority of a federal court.

There is no suggestion in this statement that the school board's "broad discretionary power" to prescribe a ratio of Negro to white students in each school reflecting the population of the district as a whole is limited to establishing a "goal" or a "starting point," or that it can be exercised only during a transitional period to dismantle a previously segregated school system. Moreover, the Court seems to sanction, or at least to exclude from judicial review, a breath-taking range of social experimentation by school boards, such as racial quotas and percentages derived from statistical ratios other than the black fraction of local population, as well as pupil assignments based on religion and other group characteristics that are significant in a pluralistic society. Whether the Court's observation is given its fullest potential, or is limited to the context of state-imposed segregation, it can hardly be based on the premise that school boards are the only agencies of government with discretionary authority in this area or that school enrollment ratios are the only permissible means of coping with the consequences of segregation. If the Court extends its tolerance of school-board action to legislative efforts to foster a successful pluralistic society, it might well hold that a program of black reparations was within the discretionary authority of the people's representatives.

A suggestive analogy is the decision of Congress, in the Voting Rights Act of 1965, to override state laws requiring voters to demonstrate an ability to read and write English when applied to persons educated in "American-flag schools in which the predominant classroom language was other than English." The primary beneficiaries of the legislation were Puerto Ricans barred from voting in New York by their inability to pass an English literacy test. In *Katzenbach v. Morgan,* upholding the legislation as a proper exercise of Congressional authority under Section 5 of the Fourteenth Amendment ("The Congress shall have power to enforce, by appropriate legislation, the provisions of this article"), the Supreme Court distinguished between the self-executing scope of the equal-protection clause and the discretionary authority of Congress under Section 5, and held that even if the New York literacy test did not violate the equal-protection clause, it was nevertheless a proper target for Congressional legislation. (This point is similar to the observation in the *Charlotte-Mecklenburg* case that a school board could properly take action "to prepare students to live in a pluralistic society" even if, for want of a prior constitutional violation of the equal-protection clause, the courts would not order the board to do so.) Despite the fact that voting qualifications are ordinarily prescribed by state law, the Court held that Congress could intervene if it thought that enlarging the right of Puerto Ricans residing in New York to vote would aid them "in gaining nondiscriminatory treatment in public services for the entire Puerto Rican community." In response to New York's claim that its English literacy requirement was a reasonable way to insure intelligent exercise of the franchise, the Court said:

> It was well within congressional authority to say that [the] need of the Puerto Rican minority for the vote warranted federal intrusion upon any state interests served by the English literacy requirement. It was for Congress, as the branch that made this judgment, to assess and weigh the various conflicting considerations—the risk or pervasiveness of the discrimination in governmental services, the effectiveness of eliminating the state restriction on the right to vote as a means of dealing with the evil, the adequacy or availability of alternative remedies, and the nature and significance of the state interests that would be affected by the nullification of the English literacy requirement as applied to residents who have successfully completed the sixth grade in a Puerto Rican school. It is not for us to review the congressional resolution of these factors. It is enough that we be able to perceive a basis upon which the Congress might resolve the conflict as it did.[115]

Compared with black reparations, the Congressional legislation upheld in *Katzenbach v. Morgan* was in one respect more difficult to square with the Constitution. The states have primary power to prescribe the qualifications for voting in state elections;[116] the authority of Congress to supersede state laws—"federal intrusion," in the Court's phrase—is clearly secondary. In *Katzenbach v. Morgan,* the federal restriction on New York's literacy test was held to be "appropriate legislation" to enforce the Fourteenth Amendment (and hence authorized by Section 5 of the amendment), even though the Court was prepared to assume that the test itself was not unconstitutional. By contrast, a federal program of black reparations would not trench upon the rights of the states in any way and would be intended as compensation for a century of state and federal violations of the equal-protection clause. Moreover, it would rest not only on the limited authority granted to Congress by Section 5 of the Fourteenth Amendment, but also on the broad and primary power of Congress to "provide for . . . the general Welfare of the United States." As I pointed out at the beginning of this chapter, in establishing federal spending programs Congress routinely—indeed, unavoidably—decides who may and who may not receive benefits; and the judiciary rarely overrides this legislative judgment.

Predictions are perilous in so unexplored an area, but the Supreme Court's endorsement of racial classifications in its recent school desegregation opinions goes a long way—an unexpectedly long way—toward the acceptance of a "remedial" racial code. The likelihood of judicial tolerance would probably be heightened if the issue is whether a code promulgated by the legislature is a permissible exercise of its discretionary authority, rather than whether a court on its own motion should compel a racial code to be used by another branch of the government. I must confess, however, to a residual doubt, arising because the Supreme Court has not yet seized the nettle of individual racial classifications. To be concrete: when a school board uses a racial quota or percentage as a "starting point," as permitted if not directed by the *Charlotte-Mecklenburg* case, can it properly compel the pupils to disclose their individual racial composition, investigate the truth of their assertions, and impose a penalty for misrepresentation? Or does the Court assume that compliance with its mandate is to be achieved only by the relaxed modes of racial identification now in vogue, such as the visual impressions of teachers and administrators, and pupil questionnaries that carry no penalty for erroneous claims?

The Court might conclude that estimates, surveys, questionnaires, and other casual methods of determining racial percentages are either so unreliable or so susceptible to manipulation that more formal modes are reasonable or even necessary, however distasteful their use may be. This conclusion would be approved by those who think that a desire for personal privacy in this area is uncommon, contemptible, or both. On the other hand, the Court might forbid the use of compulsory individual classifications, especially if it thought that the debatable cases would be so few that a rough estimate of compliance would be almost as accurate as an exact body count. This factual assumption might well be true of school desegregation plans, but for the reasons canvassed in Chapter 10 ("Identifying the Beneficiaries"), it would be all but impossible to administer a program of individual black reparations without an official procedure for classifying the claimants by race.

Another qualification to be attached to my already guarded conclusion is that the program, even if otherwise constitutionally acceptable, would have to be corrective, imposing racial restrictions only to cure the evils stimulating their adoption. This would imply that the program's benefits, time scale, and other characteristics would be subject to a residual power of judicial review, lest its racial qualifications outlive their justification. A similar point was made in the Court's opinion in the *Charlotte-Mecklenburg* case:

> Neither school authorities nor district courts are constitutionally required to make year-by-year adjustments of the racial composition of student bodies once the affirmative duty to desegregate has been accomplished and racial discrimination through official action is eliminated from the system. . . . [I]n the absence of a showing that either the school authorities or some other agency of the State has deliberately attempted to fix or alter demographic patterns to affect the racial composition of the schools, further intervention by a district court should not be necessary.[117]

As one surveys life in America today, however, the day seems unfortunately far off when one will be able to say that the consequences of segregation and other forms of official discrimination have so totally evaporated that remedial action has become an anachronism.

As a lawyer, I have not been able to hold back these observations on the constitutional status of black reparations. In the end, however, a judicial verdict rejecting the program's constitutionality would not be a judgment on its fairness or wisdom. If the Constitution does not now permit reparations, it could be amended to remove the barrier. Conversely, if a constitutional amendment is not needed, so that Congress now has the power to enact a program of black reparations, the wisdom of doing so remains an open question. Congress does not and should not do everything that it is free to do. In Chapter 10 I set out my misgivings about the use of a racial code and individual racial classifications in a program of black reparations, as well as my parallel doubts about the use of black groups as conduits or intermediaries. If these dangers are as substantial as I have suggested, they would not be eliminated by a judicial decision upholding such a program's constitutionality.

12.

Black Reparations, Justice, and Social Welfare

The United States is besieged by a host of public ills—poverty, racial inequality, crime, educational failures, environmental pollution, housing shortages, soaring health costs, and the breakdown of urban services. Money alone will not cure these social diseases, and even if it is applied in combination with all the talent, energy, and imagination that we can muster, the cure may still elude us. Without vastly increased public expenditures, however, there is no prospect of stabilizing these disorders, let alone alleviating them. To this agenda of domestic needs, most would add a call for emergency assistance to foreign countries gripped by famine, drought, or war (including aid to Vietnam on a scale commensurate with our contribution to its devastation), and a more continuous effort to combat disease, malnutrition, low productivity, and other endemic deficiencies of underdeveloped countries. Urgent as these needs are, however, a realistic assessment of the future requires one to acknowledge that only a modest fraction of our national resources will be devoted to these public purposes. This means that proposals for black reparations must compete with other claims of no mean scale.

I do not suggest that a fixed amount or percentage of our gross national product has somehow been unalterably ear-marked for all of these claims in the aggregate, so that every dollar allocated to one must be diverted from the others. The fraction of national resources devoted to public needs obvi-ously fluctuates in response to a myriad of moral, social, and political pressures; and new demands may elicit increased support. Just as people who customarily contribute to one charity may be the best targets for the campaign of another charitable group, so a nation that already devotes large amounts to social problems may be more ready to enlarge its agenda than one with equal resources but a less responsive tradition. If the financial demands of our social problems seem insatiable, however, the reaction may come to be a shrugging of shoulders, with the comment that human mis-ery is the will of Allah.

In Chapter 2 ("The Case for Compensation"), I offered an argument in support of a program of black reparations, but did not attempt to compare it with competing demands. I now turn to the question: Where do black reparations fit into this framework of limited resources and enormous needs? To move the issue from an abstract to a "hard" context, it may be helpful to look at the National Urban Coalition's recent "Counterbudget," proposed as a "blueprint for changing na-tional priorities" within "the realities of the federal budget and the American economy."[118] This study calls for an in-crease in federal expenditures from the $213 billion estimated for 1971 (out of a gross national product of $1,004 billion) to

$353 billion in 1976 (with an estimated GNP of $1,489 billion). The principal areas of change proposed by the National Urban Coalition are:

	Amount (billions)
Employment and manpower training	$ 5.6
Income maintenance: social insurance	35.6
Income maintenance: income support	28.7
Health	51.6
Education	11.1
Fiscal relief for states and localities	9.6
Metropolitan development	6.3
Housing	2.1
Law enforcement and criminal justice	2.9
National defense and military assistance (decrease)	(24.1)
Foreign economic assistance	4.4
Interest on debt	9.2
Postal service (decrease)	(2.0)
NET CHANGE	$141.0

Because this "Counterbudget" is far from radical, and was indeed criticized by some of those consulted by its authors as lacking in boldness and farsightedness, it has a twofold significance in this discussion of black reparations. As a modest estimate of widely felt needs reflecting "establishment liberalism," it can be regarded as a minimum list of proposed expenditures with which a program of black reparations must compete; and its very modesty simultaneously acknowledges and reminds us that increased federal expenditures on social needs must overcome enormous political resistance.

These harsh facts would not be an obstacle to a purely symbolic program of black reparations: a national park, monument, or cultural institution could be financed without impairing the priority of other social claims; and this would also be true of some special-purpose programs, such as a university or research center. Black reparations that seriously endeavored to close the economic gap between blacks and whites, however, would move us to an entirely different level of magnitude. I have not previously tried to put a price tag on such a program, and would have preferred to leave this job to a staff of qualified economists and other experts. Lacking their assistance, however, I am impelled to strike out on my own. As one possibility, we might multiply the 1969 gap between black and white per capita income ($1,510) by the number of blacks (22.5 million), and take the resulting amount ($34 billion) as a rough estimate of the annual cost of a reparations program.[119] For a similarly rough estimate of the program's duration, it would probably be realistic to assume that the income gap to be bridged by reparations will be gradually narrowed by independent social and economic forces, but will continue at a significant level for at least a decade or two.[120]

This estimate assumes that the entire gap between black and white average earnings is attributable to racial discrimination, or at least that it can be provisionally attributed to this cause, pending the filtering out by a more adequate study[121] of such influences as age and geographical location. But it disregards differences in the current net worth of blacks and whites, and therefore would not rectify the accumulated effect of depressed earning capacity in past years. The only available estimate of the black net-worth "gap," computed as of 1967, is $32.6 billion.[122] The inadequacy of *current* income disparities as a measure of black reparations becomes apparent when we note that the income of blacks and whites at the bottom of the economic ladder is equalized by welfare payments; but this does not neutralize the lingering impact of segregation and discrimination on the economic well-being of a black now on welfare whose income would have been higher than the welfare level (in the past, now, or in the future). Indeed, not even an instantaneous and permanent elimination of the current gap between white and black income at every level would eliminate the accumulated disparity. Freedom now, in short, is not the same as freedom yesterday.

These estimates of the disparities in current income and net worth between black and white Americans do not include any allowance for the humiliation inflicted by segregation. The problem of converting emotional injury into money was discussed earlier. No attempt was made there to calculate the aggregate amount that might be awarded if the nation undertook to compensate blacks for this type of injury, but it is plain that the cost would be enormous. Unless fashioned solely as a symbol, then, a program of black reparations would have to fight for room on the federal fiscal agenda.

Seeing black reparations as a competitor of nonracial welfare programs, welfare economists are likely to resist such proposals, and argue that public assistance and similar benefits should be based solely on economic need—starting with the most poverty-stricken members of our society and moving up the economic ladder only after those on the bottom rungs have been fully provided for. This approach calls for the award of benefits person-by-person or family-by-family in a process taking no account of racial, ethnic, or other criteria as such because it looks only to the claimant's income level. Thus, if a family of four needs $5,000 per year to live at a subsistence level, all funds appropriated for public assistance would first be channeled to families below the $5,000 level. If the society were then willing to use more of its resources for public assistance, all families at the $5,000 level would qualify for additional payments on a plane of equality. As additional resources are pledged by society to the alleviation of poverty, they would be distributed in such a way as to raise the bottom level of income.

Addressed to advocates of this principle of distributive justice, appeals on behalf of a special group fall on deaf ears. If it is argued, for example, that city people, veterans, Boy Scouts, illiterates, or cripples should be singled out for public aid, the answer would always be the same: poor city people, poor veterans, poor Boy Scouts, poor illiterates, and poor cripples will be benefited if they fall below the subsistence level; if they are above this level they must wait until funds are available to raise *everyone* from $5,000 to $6,000, from $6,000 to $7,000, and so on. (This approach would not preclude cost-of-living differentials between city and rural people, between cripples and noncripples, etc., with the result, for example, that the subsistence level might be $5,500 for city people and only $5,000 for rural people; but these adjustments would be a refinement of the basic principle, not a repudiation of it.) The same answer would be made to the demand for black reparations—viz., poor blacks share in welfare distributions along with all other poor people; the blacks who are now above sea level must wait until the *general* level of public aid is raised, when they will share in the benefits along with everyone else.

A system of social welfare constructed on this principle would be consistent, but we depart from the principle with such frequency that one may properly ask whether something is overlooked in concentrating on what the tax economist calls vertical equity, i.e., justice as between one income group and another. What has been overlooked, obviously, is the issue of horizontal equity, i.e., justice within each income group. If Jones and Smith both earn $5,000 a year but Smith has been prevented by society from earning $6,000 a year, his complaint is not adequately answered by telling him that when society is ready to help persons at the $5,000 level, he and Jones will share equally in public assistance. To be more explicit, if Smith is a war veteran with a permanent service-connected disability, it is not unfair to compensate him for the loss of potential earnings, even if he is independently wealthy, and his claim is not weakened by the fact that nothing is to be paid to Jones; indeed, equality between them may be inequity.

The same points can be made in support of a program of black reparations: it is a remedy for injustice, not a poverty program, and its objective would not be achieved by increasing public assistance or welfare benefits for everyone at the bottom of the economic ladder. More generous welfare or income-maintenance subsidies would, of course, obliterate the gap between white and black incomes at the lower levels; but this would merely illustrate the deficiency, discussed earlier, of using the traditional income gap as a measure of black reparations without compensating for past discrimination. It might also dissipate some of the steam behind demands for black reparations, though this is not a foregone conclusion; a step forward may generate the momentum for a second step rather than a desire to rest. Similarly, full employment and higher wages should help to close the gap between white and black earnings; because blacks are traditionally "last hired, first fired," they are especially susceptible to the leverage of improved general economic conditions. But here, too, uniformity of earnings for the future will not compensate for the deprivations of the past. Thus, although black reparations and nonracial welfare programs have a large overlapping constituency of lower-income blacks, they have different objectives and results; and in a context of limited resources, they compete not only with other claims but with each other.

This conclusion returns us to the starting point of this chapter. The claim for black reparations competes with other demands for public funds, which in turn depend on the way our gross national product is divided between the private sector (personal consumption, business plant and equipment, and other investment) and public expenditures. In deciding whether black reparations should be given priority over education, foreign aid, or income support, and whether these government expenditures are preferable to lower taxes, the citizen must look to his own fundamental values. Moreover, since the amount that could be spent for any of these causes is elastic, he must go beyond a mere ranking of the categories by allocating dollar amounts to each line. If I were to offer such a budget to the reader without discussing the merits of each of the competing claims (a task beyond the intended scope of this work), it would be only an arbitrary presentation of my own social and political preferences, expressed in financial terms. I content myself, therefore, with the hope that this preliminary inquiry will aid the reader in fitting the concept of black reparations into his own hierarchy of values.

A brief summary of my argument may be in order. Using Section 1983 of existing law as an example of compensation for governmental misconduct that invades the citizen's constitutional rights, I have argued that the concept of black reparations is far from bizarre or unprecedented. Ordinarily, of course, indemnity is paid only for behavior that was wrong as judged by the generally accepted legal principles when commited. But there is nothing remarkable in going beyond this practice and redressing injuries attributable to acts thought to be legal when committed, if they are condemned by a later change in legal or constitutional doctrine. Applied to segregation, this approach would suggest the payment of compensation for state-prescribed segregation in public schools and other public facilities. Compensation for violations of the "separate but equal" doctrine is even more consonant with tradition, since these violations were legally wrong even when committed.

A compensation plan limited to actual violations of the "separate but equal" doctrine and to official segregation, however, would be far from comprehensive. Millions of blacks who were not directly subject to formal segregation in the South felt the pervasive impact of official discrimination by the federal government and by states and other governmental agencies in the North. A program of black reparations that excluded these blacks would be unfair, but to include them would create still other problems. Individual reparations could not be provided by the government without an official code of racial classification, while group reparations would entail a process of official favor to some black organizations and disfavor to others. Because both routes are fraught with dangers, I have used the term "a second American dilemma" to describe the situation in which we find ourselves.

The validity of this label will, of course, be denied by those who perceive no adverse consequences from a program of reparations to black organizations or to individual blacks, as well as by those who think I have exaggerated the side effects of such a program. The "dilemma" will also seem nonexistent to those who reject the idea of reparations because, in their view, the injury resulting from segregation is too difficult to assess, too great to be susceptible to compensation, or too similar to other wrongs that go uncompensated in an imperfect world. We are, or ought to be, at the beginning of a national debate on these questions. I have sought to open the discussion, not to close it.

Notes

CHAPTER 1

1. The Freedmen's Bureau administered a wide range of services (food, housing, education, medical care, etc.) to Southerners, black and white, displaced by the Civil War and emancipation; but in neither theory nor practice did it provide compensation to the ex-slaves. Even in the Reconstruction legislatures of the short-lived "Radical South," public welfare programs were modest and did not include reparations to the ex-slaves. See George R. Bentley, *A History of the Freedmen's Bureau* (University of Pennsylvania Press, 1955); John H. Franklin, *Reconstruction: After the Civil War* (University of Chicago Press, 1961), pp. 114–15, 139–41; Kenneth M. Stampp, *The Era of Reconstruction, 1865 1877* (Vintage, 1967), pp. 122–35.
2. The Black Manifesto is reprinted in Appendix A. For Forman's account of the Black Manifesto, see his *The Making of Black Revolutionaries* (Macmillan, 1972, pp. 543–50).

139

3. See *New York Times,* for the following dates in 1961: May 6, pp. 36–37; May 15, p. 22; May 18, pp. 30, 80; May 23, p. 24; May 25, p. 66; June 6, p. 24; June 12, p. 63; June 30, p. 30; July 7, p. 20; July 13, p. 68; July 27, p. 1; Sept. 15, p. 1; Sept. 27, p. 36; Nov. 14, p. 35; and Dec. 21, p. IV–13. For a review of the situation a year after the Black Manifesto was promulgated, see *New York Times,* June 10, 1970, p. 49.

4. *New York Times,* Sept. 9, 1969.

   For more extended discussion of the Black Manifesto, see Arnold Schuchter, *Reparations* (Lippincott, 1970); and Robert S. Lecky and H. Elliott Wright (eds.), *Black Manifesto* (Sheed & Ward, 1969). Like the Black Manifesto itself, both focus on the role of religion and the churches. A more general discussion, predating the Manifesto, is Hughes, Reparations for Blacks?, 43 N.Y.U. Law Rev. 1063 (1968); see also 2 Rev. of Black Political Economy, No. 2 (special issue on reparations) (1972); Collins, The United States Owes Reparations to Its Black Citizens, 16 How. L. J. 82 (1970); Bedau, Compensatory Justice and the Black Manifesto, 56, The Monist 20 (1972); Browne, The Economic Case for Reparations to Black America, 62 Amer. Econ. Rev., Papers and Proceedings of 84th Annual meeting (1972), p. 39. For a satirical parable, see Vorspan, "A Modern Bible Story," *Saturday Review,* Aug. 16, 1969.

5. See John H. Bracey, August Meier, and Elliott Rudwick (eds.), *Black Nationalism in America* (Bobbs-Merrill, 1970), pp. 173, 180–81; Bentley, supra note 1; W. E. B. DuBois, *Black Reconstruction* (Meridian, 1964).

6. Gunnar Myrdal, *An American Dilemma* (Harper & Row, 1962), p. 225. See also Harold W. Horowitz and Kenneth L. Karst, *Law, Lawyers and Social Change* (Bobbs-Merrill, 1969), a casebook focusing on race relations, which is similarly devoid of material on reparations.

7. Otto Kuester, whose views are set forth in his *Erfahrungen in der deutschen Wiedergutmachung, Recht und Staat,*

346/347 (J. C. B. Mohr, Tübingen, 1967). See also Kurt R. Grossmann, *Die Ehrenschuld* (Berlin, 1967); Raul Hilberg, *The Destruction of the European Jews* (Quadrangle, 1967), pp. 746–59; Woodward, *Germany Makes Amends*, 31 U.S. Dept. of State Bull. 126 (1954). There is no comprehensive study in either German or English of the history, philosophy, and administration of the German restitution and reparations program (involving aggregate payments of about $4.4 billion as of 1965, according to the 1965 Annual Report of the Conference on Jewish Material Claims Against Germany); it is to be hoped that this gap will be filled before the memories of important participants now living in the United States, Germany, and Israel fade or are stilled by death. For the Italian counterpart of the German program, which embraces anti-fascists as well as Jews, see Enzo Capalozza, Gli assegni pensionistici ai perseguitati politici antifascisti e razziali e il problema della giurisdizione, Rassegna sanitaria, n.5 maggio 1959, pp. 3–15; Alberto Petreni, Osservazioni sulla revoca e la riduzione di donazioni eseguite da israeliti colpiti dalle disposizioni razziali, Giurisprudenza italiana, 1962, p. IV, pp. 99–112.

CHAPTER 2

8. Martin L. King, Jr., *Why We Can't Wait* (Harper & Row, 1964), p. 152.
9. Jim Marketti, *Black Equity in the Slave Industry* (Industrial Relations Research Institute, University of Wisconsin, 1969), p. 15, also in 2 Rev. of Black Pol. Econ., No. 2, p. 43 (1972). By the same standard, Marketti would find Forman too modest, since even if his demand is expanded to a fraction of gross national product corresponding to the $500 million demanded of religious groups alone, it would be only $62.5 billion. See also Robert W. Fogel and Stanley L. Engerman, *The Economics of Slavery*, citing prior studies, in Fogel and

Engerman (eds.), *The Reinterpretation of American Economic History* (Harper & Row, 1971), p.311; Alfred H. Conrad and John R. Meyer, *The Economics of Slavery* (Aldine, 1964).

10. Robert Penn Warren, *Who Speaks for the Negro?* (Vintage, 1965), pp. 434–35. See also Bayard Rustin, *New York Times,* May 9, 1969, p. 44: "If my great-grandfather picked cotton for 50 years, then he may deserve some money, but he's dead and nobody owes me anything." See also infra note 32.

11. T. T. Fortune, *Black and White* (Arno, 1968), pp. 179, 195.

12. C. Vann Woodward, *The Strange Career of Jim Crow,* 2d ed. (Oxford, 1957), pp. 7–8. See also Charles S. Johnson, *Backgrounds to Patterns of Negro Segregation* (Crowell, 1970), a summary of staff studies of white–black relations on the eve of World War II, prepared for Gunnar Myrdal's *An American Dilemma,* supra note 6.

13. 163 U.S. 537, at 544, 549, and 550 (1896). The informal designation of separate streets for blacks and whites, however, was not unknown. See Vernon Lane Wharton, *The Negro in Mississippi 1865–1890* (Torchbooks, 1965), pp. 232–33.

14. 163 U.S. at 560 and 562. See also, p. 577:

> Everyone knows that the statute in question had its origin in the purpose, not so much to exclude white persons from railroad cars occupied by blacks, as to exclude colored people from coaches occupied by or assigned to white persons. . . . The thing to accomplish was, under the guise of giving equal accommodation for whites and blacks, to compel the latter to keep to themselves while travelling in railroad passenger coaches. No one would be so wanting in candor as to assert the contrary.

For an eloquent statement of the contemporary meaning of segregation, see Black, The Lawfulness of the Segregation Decisions, 69 Yale L. J. 421 (1960).

15. John A. Garraty, *Quarrels That Have Shaped the Constitution* (Harper & Row, 1964), pp. 150, 152.

16. See note 46 infra.
17. See note 12 supra; see also Wynes, The Evolution of Jim Crow Laws in Twentieth-Century Virginia, 28 Phylon 416 (1967). According to Louis R. Harlan, *Separate and Unequal* (University of North Carolina Press, 1958), p. 259, the gap between white and Negro school opportunities in the South reached its broadest about 1930. For a summary of Jim Crow laws and regulations, see Charles S. Mangum, Jr., *The Legal Status of the Negro* (University of North Carolina Press, 1940), pp. 181–222; Morroe Berger, *Equality by Statute* (Anchor, 1968); Pauli Murray, *State Laws on Race and Color* (Woman's Division of Christian Service, Methodist Church, 1950, Supp. 1955).
18. Hawkins v. Town of Shaw, 437 F.2d 1286 (5th Cir. 1971).
19. Carr v. Corning, 182F.2d 14, 17–19 (D.C. Cir. 1950); D.C. Code, Section 31–1111 (West 1968), which provides that

> Any white resident shall be privileged to place his or her child or ward at any one of the schools provided for the education of white children in the District of Columbia that he or she may think proper to select, with the consent of the Board of Education; and any colored resident shall have the same rights with respect to colored schools.

20. See Samuel Krislov, *The Negro in Federal Employment* (University of Minnesota Press, 1967), p.23; Wolgemuth, Woodrow Wilson and Federal Segregation, 44 J. Negro History 158 (1959); Ulysses Lee, The Employment of Negro Troops (Special Study, U. S. Army in World War II, Office of the Chief of Military History, U.S. Army, 1966); Billington, Freedom to Serve: The President's Committee on Equality of Treatment and Opportunity in the Armed Forces, 1949 1950, 51 J. Negro History 262 (1966); Dalifiume, The Fahy Committee and Desegregation of the Armed Forces, 31 The Historian 1 (1968).
21. Swann v. Charlotte-Mecklenburg Board of Education, 402 U.S. 1, at 13. The 1968 and 1969 cases mentioned in the text

are: Green v. County School Board, 391 U.S. 430 (1968), and Alexander v. Holmes County Board of Education, 396 U.S. 19 (1969).

22. Philip S. Foner (ed.), *The Life and Writings of Frederick Douglass* (International Publishers, 1950–55), Vol. 4, p. 316.

23. Bivens v. Six Unknown Agents of the Federal Bureau of Narcotics, 403 U.S. 388 (1971); see generally Dellinger, Of Rights and Remedies: The Constitution as a Sword, 85 Harv. L. Rev. 1532 (1972). A troublesome issue of official immunity remained to be decided, along with the question of actual damages, and the case was remanded by the Supreme Court for further appropriate proceedings. See also Katz, The Jurisprudence of Remedies: Constitutional Legality and the Law of Torts in Bell v. Hood, 117 U. Pa. L. Rev. 1 (1968); Hill, Constitutional Remedies, 69 Col. L. Rev. 1109 (1969); Moragne v. States Marine Lines, Inc., 398 U.S. 375 (1970) (maritime law precedent of almost ninety years' standing overruled by decision holding that compensation must be paid for wrongful death).

24. Harper and James, *The Law of Torts*, Sections 29.8–29.10 (Little, Brown, 1956), pp. 1632–46; see also Note, But What About the Victim? The Forsaken Man in American Criminal Law, 22 U. Fla. L Rev. 1 (1969); Wolfgang, Victim Compensation in Crimes of Personal Violence, 50 Minn. L. Rev. 223, 230 (1965); Note, Compensation of Persons Erroneously Confined by the State, 118 U. Pa. L. Rev. 1091 (1970).

25. This is not the place to discuss the burgeoning suggestions for reparations to women, whose status was compared by Myrdal to that of Negroes (supra note 6, at Appendix 5, pp.1073 ff.). But proposals to transfer money from men to their mothers, wives, and daughters raise important questions not posed by reparations to blacks. Moreover, "female reparations" would have to rest on arguments different from those presented here in favor of black reparations, until legal restrictions on women are condemned by a decision comparable to *Brown v. Board of Education*—an event that is not

regarded as likely in the near future by the leading commentators, Brown, Emerson, Falk, and Freedman, The Equal Rights Amendment: A Constitutional Basis for Equal Rights for Women, 80 Yale L.J. 871, 882 (1971). Reed v. Reed, 404 U.S. 71 (1971) (statutory preference for men over women in appointment of administrators of intestate estates held unconstitutional), decided after publication of their article, may show which way the winds of doctrine are blowing, but by itself it hardly disproves their prediction.

26. Justice Frankfurter, dissenting in Hensley v. Union Planters Nat'l Bank, 335 U.S. 595, at 600 (1949).

27. The statutory reference is 25 U.S.C. Section 70a (1946). See Miami Tribe v. U.S., 281 F.2d 202 (Ct. Cl. 1960), cert. denied, 366 U.S. 924 (1961); Osage Nation v. U.S., 97 F. Supp. 381 (Ct. Cl. 1951), cert. denied, 342 U.S. 896 (1951); Wilkinson, Indian Tribal Claims Before the Court of Claims, 55 Geo. L.J. 511 (1966).

28. Justice Harlan, in *Mackey v. United States,* 401 U.S. 667, at 681 (1971).

29. Williams v. United States, 401 U.S. 646 (1971; for commentary on the problem, see citations at pp.651–52 n. 3; see also Appendix to United States v. Liguori, 438 F.2d 663, 670 (2d Cir. 1971).

30. Shelley v. Kraemer, 334 U.S. 1 (1948).

31. See pp. 10–11 supra. One would wish to compare post-emancipation developments in the United States with those elsewhere, and especially in South and Central America. But see Magnus Moerner, *Race and Class in Latin America* (Columbia University Press, 1970), p. 218, asserting that aside from a few studies, "the post-abolition conditions of the Negro in Latin America remain little known"; see also Carl N. Degler, *Neither Black Nor White: Slavery and Race Relations in Brazil and the United States* (Macmillan, 1971).

32. "The Failure of Black Separatism," *Harper's,* Jan. 1970, 25, p. 31. He goes on to assert: "It is insulting to Negroes to offer them reparations for past generations of suffering, as if the

balance of an irreparable past could be set straight with a
handout." See also supra note 10.

33. Supra note 10.

CHAPTER 3

34. Supra note 23.
35. For a comprehensive survey of Section 1983's scope, see
    Emerson, Haber and Dorsen, *Political and Civil Rights in the
    United States,* 3d. ed., (Little, Brown, 1967), Vol. 2, pp. 1447–
    1454; see also Mitchum v. Foster, 92 S. Ct. 2151, 2160 et seq.
    (1972) (history of Section 1983).
36. 365 U.S. 167 (1961). Justice Harlan and Justice Stewart
    thought that the issue was "very close indeed," joining in the
    majority view primarily because two earlier cases had at-
    tributed the same meaning to a substantially identical phrase
    contained in Section 242 of Title 18, infra note 40. Justice
    Frankfurter dissented.
37. Note, Limiting the Section 1983 Action in the Wake of
    Monroe v. Pape, 82 Harv. L. Rev. 1486 (1969); Chevigny,
    Section 1983 Jurisdiction: A Reply, 83 Harv. L. Rev. 1352
    (1970); Shapo, Constitutional Tort: Monroe v. Pape, and the
    Frontiers Beyond, 60 Nw. U.L. Rev 277 (1965).
38. 365 U.S. at 248, 246. See the similar theory advanced in a
    dissent in Screws v. United States, 325 U.S. 91 (1945) (in
    which Frankfurter joined), to the effect that federal law
    (there Section 242) "was directed against those, and only
    against those, who were not punishable by State law precisely
    because they acted in obedience to unconstitutional State law
    and by State law justified their action." (Emphasis added.)

CHAPTER 4

39. For a discussion, set in a broader context, of the distinction
    between "the whole army of remedies for making prospective
    'declaration' as to the legality of [official] action" and reme-

dies for "injuries (accrued losses) arising out of official mis-conduct or the ultra vires exercise of power for which prospective declaration affords inadequate relief," see Louis L. Jaffe, *Judicial Control of Administrative Action* (Little, Brown, 1965), pp.236 ff.

40. When originally enacted (as Section 2 of the Civil Rights Act of 1866), Section 242 was narrower than Section 1983, applying primarily to deprivations of rights secured or protected by the Civil Rights Act of 1866 itself, not to all rights secured or protected by the federal Constitution or statutes. This aspect of Section 242 was broadened in 1874, and the term "willfully" was added in 1909. In one respect, Section 242 is broader than Section 1983, since it covers an invasion of the rights of any "inhabitant" of a state, whether he is a citizen or not. See United States v. Williams, 341 U.S. 70 (1951).

41. Supra note 38, at 92.

42. 365 U.S. at 187. For other formulations, see Justice Frankfurters's comment, 365 U.S. at 254, that Section 1983 would apply to a "custodian of a public building who turns out a Negro pursuant to a local ordinance"; Lane v. Wilson, 307 U.S. 268 (1939), described by Justice Brennan, in the *Adickes* case, 398 U.S. 144, 232–33 (1970), as imposing liability for damages upon state election officials "who merely carried out their official duty to prevent the plaintiffs from voting under discriminatory state statutes which made them ineligible to vote."

43. Pierson v. Ray, 386 U.S. 547, 555 (1967); see also infra note 64.

44. I have been informed by counsel (Carl Rachlin, Esq.), that no attempt was made to retry the cases following the Supreme Court's decision.

45. Supra note 13.

46. Leflar and Davis, Segregation in the Public Schools—1953, 67 Harv. L. Rev. 377 (1954).

47. Monroe v. Pape, supra note 36, at 207 (Frankfurter, J., dissenting).

48. 349 U.S. 294 (1955).
49. See Professor Bickel's comment, in Vern Countryman (ed.), *Discrimination and the Law* (University of Chicago, 1965), pp. 55, 74, that, as a general principle, "no one is under an obligation to carry out a rule of constitutional law announced by the [Supreme] Court until someone else has conducted a successful litigation and obtained a decree directing him to do so." On the necessity of exhausting administrative remedies before suing under Section 1983, see Note, Federal Judicial Review of State Welfare Practices, 67 Colum. L. Rev. 84, 104–106 (1967).
50. Green v. Country School Board, 391 U.S. 430, 438 (1968).
51. Supra note 21.

CHAPTER 5

52. See McArthur v. Pennington, 253 F. Supp. 420 (E.D. Tenn. 1963) (municipal immunity waived to extent of insurance coverage).
53. 16 Stat. 431 (1871).
54. See, for example, Adickes v. S. H. Kress & Co., 398 U.S. 144 (1970).
55. Supra note 36.
56. Avins (ed.), *The Reconstruction Amendments' Debates*, reprint of relevant portions of the Congressional debates (Virginia Commission on Constitutional Government, Richmond, 1967), p. 569.
57. Supra note 56, p. 568 (emphasis supplied).
58. For a more cautious suggestion—that Section 1983 should be interpreted to permit injunctive relief (but not damage actions) against municipalities—see Note, Injunctive Relief Against Municipalities Under Section 1983, 119 U. Pa. L. Rev. 389 (1970); Carter v. Carlson, 447 F.2d 358 (D.C.Cir.1971) (District of Columbia not exempt; see also suggestion that only municipalities clothed with immunity

by state government are exempt under Monroe v. Pape); see also infra note 63.

59. See Adickes v. S. H. Kress & Co., supra note 54; Note, The Supreme Court, 1969 Term, 84 Harv. L. Rev. 32, 71–82 (1970); Note, Adickes v. Kress: An Examination of "Under Color of . . . Custom," 66 Nw. L. Rev. 570 (1971).

60. See supra note 42.

61. Avins, supra note 56, p. 567.

62. *Id.*

63. E.g., Williford v. California, 352 F.2d 474 (9th Cir. 1965); but see Harkless v. Sweeny Independent School District, 427 F.2d 319, 321–323 (5th Cir. 1970), cert. denied, 400 U.S. 991 (1971), holding that Monroe v. Pape was concerned only with "the issue of damages against municipalities under respondeat superior," and thus implying at least the possibility that public agencies are "persons" under Section 1983 in damage actions for authorized misconduct. If Section 1983 is construed to permit suits against the state as such, its constitutional status depends upon whether it can be reconciled with the Eleventh Amendment, which has been interpreted to forbid not only suits by citizens of one state against another state but also suits against the plaintiff's own state. The bearing of the Fourteenth Amendment, and especially Section 5 thereof, on this question, is complex and unsettled. See Justice Brennan's extensive discussion in Perez v. Ledesma, 401 U.S. 82, at 104–20 (1971); Parden v. Terminal Ry., 377 U.S. 184 (1964); David P. Currie, Federal Courts (West Publ. Co. 1968), pp. 470–92; Goldberg v. Kelly, 397 U.S. 254 (1970) (injunction granted against state officials having the effect of requiring state to continue welfare payments pending hearing); Kates and Kouba, Liability of Public Entities Under Section 1983 of the Civil Rights Act, 45 So. Calif. L. Rev. 131 (1972).

64. Supra note 43, at 553; see Kates, Immunity of State Judges Under the Federal Civil Rights Acts: Pierson v. Ray Reconsidered, 65 Nw. L. Rev. 615 (1970).

65. 341 U.S. 367 (1951).
66. Avins, supra note 56, at 554.
67. For a discussion of this distinction, traditionally applied more frequently in determining the tort liability of municipalities than that of states, see Harper and James, supra note 24, Secs. 29.4–29.6. For another formulation, distinguishing between functions that only a state can carry on and those that can be conducted by either public or private agencies, see New York v. United States, 326 U.S. 572 (1946).
68. Bell v. Hood, 327 U.S. 678, 684 (1946).

CHAPTER 6

69. Supra note 36 at 196, n.5. Segregated schools may be preferred by some blacks as a device, temporary or permanent, to inculcate racial unity and pride. See, for example, W.E.B. Dubois, Does the Negro Need Separate Schools? 4 J. Negro Educ. 328 (1935). But pre-1954 segregation is another matter.
70. Infra note 119.
71. Harper and James, supra note 24, Section 25.8.
72. United States v. Wood, Wire & Metal Lathers Int'l Union, 328 F.Supp. 429 (S.D.N.Y.1971).
73. Infra note 74; *New York Times,* May 6, 1970, p.1; Sostre v. McGinnis, 442 F.2d 178, note 52 (2d Cir. 1971).
74. Chicago, R.I. & P.Ry.Co. v. Allison, 178 S.W. 401 (Ark.1915) (though described as excessive by the Court, the award presumably reflected community attitudes as interpreted by the jury).
75. See W.E.B DuBois, supra note 69.
76. State liability for damages under Section 1983 is a different question from whether the behavior of these "private" organizations should be treated as "state action" for other purposes, e.g., Section 1 of the Fourteenth Amendment when unaided by legislative action under Section 5. See Peterson v. Greenville, 373 U.S. 244 (1963), and companion cases decided at the same time.

77. The Pennsylvania, 86 U.S. 125 (1874); for the less severe principles of ordinary tort law, see Harper and James, *supra* note 24, Section 20.3. See also Peterson v. City of Greenville, 373 U.S. 244 (1963) (municipal ordinance requiring segregated lunch counter precludes evidence that proprietor would have segregated customers in absence of ordinance).

CHAPTER 8

78. See note 99 *infra*.
79. Vine Deloria, Jr., *We Talk, You Listen* (Macmillan, 1970), pp. 148–49. For a more critical view of the Indian Claims Commission, see Deloria's later work, *Of Utmost Good Faith* (Straight Arrow, 1971), p. 142.
80. Deloria, *We Talk, You Listen,* *supra* note 79, pp. 45, 87–88, 94.
81. Gila River Pima-Maricopa Indian Community v. United States, 427 F. 2d 1194, 1201 (Ct. Cl. 1970) (Davis, J., concurring).
82. See note 7 *supra*; Appendix B.
83. 2 Rev. of Black Pol. Econ., No. 2, p. v (1972). The NAACP later withdrew from association with the Convention "because of a difference in ideology." *New York Times,* May 17, 1972, p. 30.
84. See Deloria, *We Talk, You Listen,* *supra* note 79, p. 72, describing his impression of the allocation by religious groups of "crisis money" in 1967 and 1968:

> The chief method of distinguishing good guys from bad guys was whether or not they believed in "confrontation." If an Indian swore he believed in "confrontation" and promised to burn the agency building when he got home, he was eligible for funds. If he was uncertain about assassinating the Secretary of the Interior, then he was classified as a "conservative racist" and was not funded.

85. See La Farge, Termination of Federal Supervision: Disintegration of the American Indians, 311 Annals of Amer. Acad. of Pol. and Soc. Sci. 41 (1957); Watkins, Termination of Federal Supervision: The Removal of Restrictions over Indian Property and Person, id. at 47; *New York Times,* June 28, 1970 (only 80 of 2133 Klamath Indians voted to remain in tribe); Alan L. Sorkin, *American Indians and Federal Aid* (The Brookings Institution, 1971), pp. 156–61; infra note 99.

86. Palmer v. Thompson, 403 U.S. 217 (1971). A discriminatory refusal to commence a public program could possibly be remedied, but the problem of proof would be formidable.

87. For remedial programs now in force, see infra note 114.

88. Donald E. Smith, *India as a Secular State* (Princeton University Press, 1963), pp.311–16. I am indebted to Marc Galanter, of the University of Chicago, for allowing me to see the manuscript of his forthcoming study, "Equality and Compensatory Discrimination in India: The Jurisprudence of Preferential Treatment."

CHAPTER 9

89. Kaplan, Equal Justice in an Unequal World: Equality For The Negro—The Problem of Special Treatment, 61 Nw. U. L. Rev. 363 (1966); see also the statement in Swann v. Charlotte-Mecklenburg Board of Education, supra note 21, p.28, that "all things are not equal in a system that has been deliberately constructed and maintained to enforce racial segregation."

CHAPTER 10

90. For a recent summary, see Richard A. Goldsby, *Race and Races* (Macmillan, 1971): "[T]he scientific notion of race is statistical and describes the characteristics of populations. It does not and cannot describe a particular individual in a

population". See also infra note 93; and note the basically cultural theory of race expounded by DuBois (men are divided "into races, which, while they perhaps transcend scientific definition, nevertheless, are clearly defined to the eye of the Historian and Sociologist"), in Bracey, Meier, and Rudwick (eds.), supra note 5, p. 252.

91. See United States Commission on Civil Rights, Federal Civil Rights Enforcement Effort (1970), pp.123–28. Mindful of the continuing danger that racial classifications will be abused, and of the independent interest in privacy, the United States Civil Service Commission, in authorizing the use of an automated procedure to process minority-group statistics, requires racial classifications to be excluded from regular personnel files and forbids supervisors from asking any individual about his racial or ethnic origin (United States Civil Service Commission, FPM Letter No. 290–2, Sept. 30, 1969). See also note 94 infra.

91a. Such a "same class" requirement was applied by the courts until the Supreme Court held in 1972 that a white defendant could make the same objection to a jury from which Negroes were arbitrarily excluded. See Peters v. Kiff, 92 S. Ct. 2163 (1972).

92. Sipes v. McGhee, 316 Mich. 614, 620, 25 N.W. 2d 638, 641 (1947) (restrictive covenant); see also State v. Treadway, 52 So. 500 (La. 1910), summarizing definitions of "negro," "mulatto," "colored," etc.; Mangum and Murray, supra note 17.

92a. United States v. Flagler County School District, 457 F.2d 1403 (5th Cir. 1972).

93. Stuckert, "Race Mixture: The African Ancestry of White Americans," in Peter B. Hammond (ed.), *Physical Anthropology and Archaeology* (Macmillan, 1964), p. 192; see also Heer, infra note 119. For an attempt to measure the "genetic distance" of American blacks from their African forbears by using morphological and serological tests, see Pollitzer, The

Negroes of Charleston (S.C.): A Study of Hemoglobin Types, Serology, and Morphology, J. Physical Anthropology, vol. 16 (N.S.), 241 (1958), and references there cited.

94. But see Justice Stewart (with whom Justice Douglas joined) in a concurring opinion in McLaughlin v. Florida, 379 U.S. 184, 198 (1964): ". . . I cannot conceive of a valid legislative purpose under our Constitution for a state law which makes the color of a person's skin the test of whether his conduct is a criminal offense"; perhaps, however, the gravamen of the offense of filing a false claim for reparations would be not the color of the claimant's skin but his misrepresentation of its color. In commenting on the use of racial classification in criminal statutes, Justice Stewart acknowledged that "[t]here might be limited room under the Equal Protection Clause for a civil law requiring the keeping of racially segregated public records for statistical or other valid purposes," citing Tancil v. Woolls, 379 U.S. 19 (1964), per curiam, affirming Hamm v. Virginia State Board of Elections, 230 F. Supp. 156 (E.D. Va. 1964), upholding the designation of race in divorce decrees, in aid of state's vital statistics.

95. Landis, South African Apartheid Legislation, 71 Yale L.J. 1 and 437 (1961 and 1962).

96. Infra note 114.

97. S. 1830, 91st Cong., 2d Sess. Section 3(f), discussed in S. Rep. No. 91–925, 91st Cong., 2d Sess. 2–3 (1970); Affiliated Ute Citizens v. United States, 92 S. Ct. 1456 (1972).

98. See supra note 92.

99. 25 U.S.C. Sections 1301–03 (1968). For a discussion of the background of this legislation and of its coverage, see Lazarus, Title II of the 1968 Civil Rights Act: An Indian Bill of Rights, 45 North Dakota L. Rev. 337 (1969); see also Groundhog v. Keeler, 442 F.2d 674, 10th Cir. 1971 (Title II not applicable to legislation authorizing presidential appointment of principal chief of Cherokee Tribe); Kennerly v. District Court, 400 U.S. 423 (1971). Decisions about tribal mem-

bership and the division of tribal property are especially prickly, reflecting a tension between self-government and the outsider's concept of fairness. See Martinez v. Southern Ute Tribe, 249 F.2d 915 (10th Cir. 1957), cert. denied, 356 U.S. 960 (1958), due process clause not applicable to denial of tribal membership; S. Rep. No. 91–1339, 91st Cong., 2d sess. (1970), pp. 13–19 (complaints by off-reservation Indians about improper tribal membership rolls, lack of notification of tribal meetings, and tribal council's failure to answer letters of inquiry); see also Colliflower v. Garland, 342 F.2d 369 (9th Cir. 1965), writ of habeas corpus to review detention by tribal court; supra note 85.

100. There is a vast literature on the application of constitutional standards to "private" organizations. See Henry J. Friendly, *The Dartmouth College Case and the Public-Private Penumbra* (Austin: University of Texas Press, 1970), included in 12 Texas Quarterly, No. 2, Supp. (1969), which cites the major earlier articles on this subject; Seidenberg v. McSorleys' Old Ale House, Inc., 317 F. Supp. 593 (S.D.N.Y. 1970).

CHAPTER 11

101. See Graham v. Richardson, 403 U.S. 365 (1971); Van Alstyne, The Demise of the Right-Privilege Distinction in Constitutional Law, 81 Harv. L. Rev. 1439 (1968).
102. Williamson v. Lee Optical Co., 348 U.S. 483, 489 (1955).
103. McGowan v. Maryland, 366 U.S. 420, 425–26 (1961).
104. Hirabayashi v. United States, 320 U.S. 81, 100 (1943).
105. Slaughter-House Cases, 83 U.S. 36, 81 (1872); see also Griffin v. Breckenridge, 403 U.S. 88 (1971) (racial background of another section of Ku Klux Act).
106. Infra note 114.
107. 71 Yale L.J. 1387 (1962).
108. Buchanan v. Warley, 245 U.S. 60 (1917).
109. Supra note 30, at 22.

110. Plessy v. Ferguson, supra note 13, at 554.

111. Supra note 21; see also the discussion of the Charlotte-Mecklenburg case by the Chief Justice in Winston-Salem/Forsyth County Board of Education v. Scott, 92 S. Ct. 1236 (1972).

112. United States v. Montgomery County Board of Education, 395 U.S. 225 (1969).

113. North Carolina State Board of Education v. Swann, 402 U.S. 43, 45–46 (1971). In the Charlotte-Mecklenburg case, supra note 21, the Court held that a somewhat comparable provision of the Civil Rights Act of 1964 ("nothing herein shall empower any official or court of the United States to issue any order seeking to achieve a racial balance in any school by requiring the transportation of pupils or students from one school to another or one school district to another in order to achieve such racial balance") had the limited function of preventing an expansion of the existing powers of courts to enforce the equal-protection clause, rather than withdrawing or restricting those powers; see also McDaniel v. Barresi, 402 U.S. 39 (1971)—the same provision does not limit the discretionary power of state school authorities.

114. For reviews of the cases, and applications to various areas, see O'Neil, Preferential Admissions: Equalizing the Access of Minority Groups to Higher Education, 80 Yale L.J. 699 (1971); Fiss, The Charlotte-Mecklenburg Case—Its Significance for Northern School Desegregation, 38 Univ. of Chi. L. Rev. 697 (1971); Fiss, A Theory of Fair Employment Laws, 38 U. Chi. L. Rev 235 (1971); Elden, "Forty Acres and a Mule," with Interest: The Constitutionality of Black Capitalism, Benign School Quotas, and other Statutory Racial Classifications, 47 J. Urban L. 591 (1969); Note, Developments in the Law—Equal Protection, 82 Harv. L. Rev. 1065, 1104–32 (1969); Note, Developments in the Law—Employment Discrimination and Title VII of the Civil Rights Act of 1964, 84 Harv. L. Rev. 1113–66; Comment, The Philadelphia Plan vs. the Chicago Plan: Alternative Approaches for Integrating

the Construction Industry, 65 Nw. L. Rev. 642 (1970); Symposium on Disadvantaged Students and Legal Education—Programs for Affirmative Action, 1970 U. of Toledo L. Rev. 277. For a vigorous criticism of the use of racial classifications in remedial legislation, see Alexander and Alexander, The New Racism: Analysis of the Use of Racial and Ethnic Criteria in Decision-Making, 9 San Diego L. Rev. 190 (1972), an analysis based primarily on concepts of justice and freedom rather than on the legal precedents ("whether or not the authorities establish the interpretations [offered by the authors] is not the point in issue; what is in issue is how the [constitutional] clauses *should* be interpreted," ibid. at 241–42).

For another straw in the wind, see Cisneros v. Corpus Christi Independent School District, 330 F. Supp. 1377 (S.D. Tex. 1971), in which a federal judge directed each party to a school desegregation case to submit "the names of 15 persons (5 Anglo, 5 Mexican-American and 5 Negroes)," from whom the court would select, by lot, a human relations committee to assist in the desegregation process.

115. Katzenbach v. Morgan, 384 U.S. 641, 653 (1966).
116. Oregon v. Mitchell, 400 U.S. 112 (1970).
117. 402 U.S., at 31–32.

CHAPTER 12

118. "National Urban Coalition," in Robert S. Benson and Harold Wolman (eds.), *Counterbudget: A Blueprint for Changing National Priorities 1971–1976* (Praeger, 1971), p. 5.
119. Computation based on 1969 statistics, U.S. Census Bureau, Social and Economic Characteristics of the Population in Metropolitan and Nonmetropolitan Areas: 1970 and 1960, Current Population Reports—Special Studies, P–23, No. 37, Table B, with family estimates converted to a per capita basis. This estimate of the aggregate gap assumes a reduction

of income for blacks who are above the average for their similarly skilled white counterparts, as well as an increase for those below the average; since a reparations program would presumably serve only the latter group, the cost of bringing them up to the white average would be larger than the $34 billion statistical gap.

For problems in estimating the size of the black population, see David M. Heer (ed.), *Social Statistics and the City* (Joint Center for Urban Studies of M.I.T. and Harvard University, 1968); see also supra note 93.

120. See generally Bureau of Census and Bureau of Labor Statistics, The Social and Economic Status of Negroes in the United States, 1970 (BLS Report No. 394, 1971); Michael J. Flax, *Blacks and Whites, An Experiment in Racial Indicators* (Urban Institute, 1971).

121. See Gary S. Becker, *The Economics of Discrimination* (University of Chicago, 1957); and a criticism of his work by Lester C. Thurow, *Poverty and Discrimination* (The Brookings Institution, 1969), pp. 112–16.

122. Mean net worth for 43,595,000 white families is estimated at $8,915; for 4,463,000 black families, at $3,096; for unrelated individuals, the comparable figures are 10,657,000 and $6,202 (white) and 1,443,000 and $1,636 (black). Gladys K. Bowles et al., Rural-Urban Migrants: 1967, A Comparison of the Demographic, Social, and Economic Characteristics of Rural-Urban Migrants with Other Population Groups, U.S. Department of Agriculture, University of Georgia, and Office of Economic Opportunity, cooperating (in process).

Appendix A

Manifesto

To
The White Christian Churches
and the Jewish Synagogues
in the United States of America
and All Other Racist Institutions

Presentation by James Forman Delivered and Adopted by the National Black Economic Development Conference in Detroit, Michigan, On April 26, 1969

159

Introduction

Total Control as the Only Solution to the Economic Problems of Black People

Brothers and Sisters:

We have come from all over the country, burning with anger and despair not only with the miserable economic plight of our people, but fully aware that the racism on which the Western World was built dominates our lives. There can be no separation of the problems of racism from the problems of our economic, political and cultural degradation. To any black man, this is clear.

But there are still some of our people who are clinging to the rhetoric of the Negro and we must separate ourselves from those Negroes who go around the country promoting all types of schemes for Black Capitalism.

Ironically, some of the most militant Black Nationalists, as they call themselves, have been the first to jump on the bandwagon of black capitalism. They are pimps; Black Power Pimps and fraudulent leaders and the people must be

161

educated to understand that any black man or Negro who is advocating a perpetuation of capitalism inside the United States is in fact seeking not only his ultimate destruction and death, but is contributing to the continuous exploitation of black people all around the world. For it is the power of the United States Government, this racist, imperialist government that is choking the life of all people around the world.

We are an African people. We sit back and watch the Jews in this country make Israel a powerful conservative state in the Middle East, but we are not concerned actively about the plight of our brothers in Africa. We are the most advanced technological group of black people in the world, and there are many skills that could be offered to Africa. At the same time, it must be publicly stated that many African leaders are in disarray themselves, having been duped into following the lines as laid out by the Western Imperialist governments.

Africans themselves succumbed to and are victims of the power of the United States. For instance, during the summer of 1967, as the representatives of SNCC, Howard Moore and I traveled extensively in Tanzania and Zambia, we talked to high, very high, governmental officials. We told them there were many black people in the United States who were willing to come and work in Africa. All these government officials who were part of the leadership in their respective governments, said they wanted us to send as many skilled people that we could contact. But this program never came into fruition and we do not know the exact reasons, for I assure you that we talked and were committed to making this a successful program. It is our guess that the United States put the squeeze on these countries, for such a program directed by SNCC would have been too dangerous to the international prestige of the U.S. It is also possible that some of the wild statements by some black leader frightened the Africans.

In Africa today, there is a great suspicion of black people in this country. This is a correct suspicion since most of the Negroes who have left the States for work in Africa usually work for the Central Intelligence Agency (CIA) or the State Department. But the respect for us as a people continues to mount and the day will come when we can return to our homeland as brothers and sisters. But we should not think of going back to Africa today, for we are located in a strategic position. We live inside the U.S. which is the most barbaric country in the world and we have a chance to help bring this government down.

Time is short and we do not have much time and it is time we stop mincing words. Caution is fine, but no oppressed people ever gained their liberation until they were ready to fight, to use whatever means necessary, including the use of force and power of the gun to bring down the colonizer.

We have heard the rhetoric, but we have not heard the rhetoric which says that black people in this country must understand that we are the Vanguard Force. We shall liberate all the people in the U.S. and we will be instrumental in the liberation of colored people in the world around. We must understand this point very clearly so that we are not trapped into diversionary and reactionary movements. Any class analysis of the U.S. shows very clearly that black people are the most oppressed group of people inside the United States. We have suffered the most from racism and exploitation, cultural degradation and lack of political power. It follows from the laws of revolution that the most oppressed will make the revolution, but we are not talking about just making the revolution. All the parties on the left who consider themselves revolutionary will say that blacks are the Vanguard, but we are saying that not only are we the Vanguard, but we must assume leadership, total control and we must exercise the humanity which is inherent in us. We are the most humane people within the U.S. We have suffered and we understand suffering. Our hearts go out to the Vietnamese for we know what it is to suffer under the domination of racist America. Our hearts, our soul and all the compassion we can mount goes out to our brothers in Africa, Santa Domingo, Latin America and Asia who are being tricked by the power structure of the U.S. which is dominating the world today. These ruthless, barbaric men have systematically tried to kill all people and organizations opposed to its imperialism. We no longer can just get by with the use of the word capitalism to describe the U.S., for it is an imperial power, sending money, missionaries and the army throughout the world to protect this government and the few rich whites who control it. General Motors and all the major auto industries are operating in South Africa, yet the white dominated leadership of the United Auto Workers sees no relationship to the exploitation of black people in South Africa and the exploitation of black people in the U.S. If they understand it, they certainly do not put it into practice which is the actual test. We as black people must be concerned with the total conditions of all black people in the world.

But while we talk of revolution which will be an armed confrontation and long years of sustained guerilla warfare inside this country, we must also talk of the type of world we want to live in. We must commit ourselves to a society where the total means of production are taken from the rich and placed into the hands of the state for the welfare of all the people. This is what we mean when we say total control. And we mean that black people who have suffered the most from exploitation and racism must move to protect their black interest by assuming leadership inside of the United States of everything that exists. The time has passed when we are second in command and the white boy stands on top. This is especially true of the Welfare Agencies in this country, but it is not enough to say that a black man is on top. He must be committed to building the new society, to taking the wealth away from the rich people such as General Motors, Ford, Chrysler, the DuPonts, the Rockefellers, the Mellons, and all the other rich white exploiters and racists who run this world.

Where do we begin? We have already started. We started the moment we were brought to this country. In fact, we started on the shores of Africa, for we have always resisted attempts to make us slaves and now we must resist the attempts to make us capitalists. It is the financial interest of the U.S. to make us capitalist, for this will be the same line as that of integration into the mainstream of American life. Therefore, brothers and sisters, there is no need to fall into the trap that we have to get an ideology. We HAVE an ideology. Our fight is against racism, capitalism and imperialism and we are dedicated to building a socialist society inside the United States where the total means of production and distribution are in the hands of the State and that must be led by black people, by revolutionary blacks who are concerned about the total humanity of this world. And, therefore, we obviously are different from some of those who seek a black nation in the United States, for there is no way for that nation to be viable if in fact the United States remains in the hands of white racists. Then too, let us deal with some statements that we should share power with whites. We say that there must be a revolutionary black Vanguard and that white people in this country must be willing to accept black leadership, for that is the only protection that black people have to protect ourselves from racism rising again in this country.

Racism in the U.S. is so pervasive in the mentality of whites that only an armed, well-disciplined, black-controlled government can insure the stamping out of racism in this country. And that is why we plead with black people not to be talking about a few crumbs, a few thousand dollars for this cooperative, or a thousand dollars which splits black people into fighting over the dollar. That is the intention of the government. We say . . . think in terms of total control of the U.S. Prepare ourselves to seize state power. Do not hedge, for time is short and all around the world, the forces of liberation are directing their attacks against the U.S. It is a powerful country, but that power is not greater than that of black people. We work the chief industries in this country and we could cripple the economy while the brothers fought guerrilla warfare in the streets. This will take some long range planning, but whether it happens in a thousand years is of no consequence. It cannot happen unless we start. How then is all of this related to this conference?

First of all, this conference is called by a set of religious people, Christians, who have been involved in the exploitation and rape of black people since the country was founded. The missionary goes hand in hand with the power of the states. We must begin seizing power wherever we are and we must say to the planners of this conference that you are no longer in charge. We the people who have assembled here thank you for getting us here, but we are going to assume power over the conference and determine from this moment on the direction in which we want it to go. We are not saying that the conference was planned badly. The staff of the conference has worked hard and have done a magnificent job in bringing all of us together and we must include them in the new membership which must surface from this point on. The conference is now the property of the people who are assembled here. This we proclaim as fact and not rhetoric and there are demands that we are going to make and we insist that the planners of this conference help us implement them.

We maintain we have the revolutionary right to do this. We have the same rights, if you will, as the Christians had in going into Africa and raping our Motherland and bringing us away from our continent of peace and into this hostile and alien environment where we have been living in perpetual warfare since 1619.

Our seizure of power at this conference is based on a program and our program is contained in the following MANIFESTO:

Black Manifesto

We the black people assembled in Detroit, Michigan for the National Black Economic Development Conference are fully aware that we have been forced to come together because racist white America has exploited our resources, our minds, our bodies, our labor. For centuries we have been forced to live as colonized people inside the United States, victimized by the most vicious, racist system in the world. We have helped to build the most industrial country in the world.

We are therefore demanding of the white Christian churches and Jewish synagogues which are part and parcel of the system of capitalism, that they begin to pay reparations to black people in this country. We are demanding $500,000,000 from the Christian white churches and the

Jewish synagogues. This total comes to 15 dollars per nigger. This is a low estimate for we maintain there are probably more than 30,000,000 black people in this country. $15 a nigger is not a large sum of money and we know that the churches and synagogues have a tremendous wealth and its membership, white America, has profited and still exploits around the world is aided and abetted by the white Christian churches and synagogues. This demand for $500,000,000 is not an idle resolution or empty words. Fifteeen dollars for every black brother and sister in the United States is only a beginning of the reparations due us as people who have been exploited and degraded, brutalized, killed and persecuted. Underneath all of this exploitation, the racism of this country has produced a psychological effect upon us that we are beginning to shake off. We are no longer afraid to demand our full rights as a people in this decadent society.

We are demanding $500,000,000 to be spent in the following way:

1. We call for the establishment of a Southern land bank to help our brothers and sisters who have to leave their land because of racist pressure [and?] for people who want to establish cooperative farms, but who have no funds. We have seen too many farmers evicted from their homes because they have dared to defy the white racism of this country. We need money for land. We must fight for massive sums of money for this Southern Land Bank. We call for $200,-000,000 to implement this program.

2. We call for the establishment of four major publishing and printing industries in the United States to be funded with ten million dollars each. These publishing houses are to be located in Detroit, Atlanta, Los Angeles, and New York. They will help to generate capital for further cooperative investments in the black community, provide jobs and an

alternative to the white-dominated and controlled printing field.

3. We call for the establishment of four of the most advanced scientific and futuristic audio-visual networks to be located in Detroit, Chicago, Cleveland and Washington, D.C. These TV networks will provide an alternative to the racist propaganda that fills the current television networks. Each of these TV networks will be funded by ten million dollars each.

4. We call for a research skills center which will provide research on the problems of black people. This center must be funded with no less than 30 million dollars.

5. We call for the establishment of a training center for the teaching of skills in community organization, photography, movie making, television making and repair, radio building and all other skills needed in communication. This training center shall be funded with no less than ten million dollars.

6. We recognize the role of the National Welfare Rights Organization and we intend to work with them. We call for ten million dollars to assist in the organization of welfare recipients. We want to organize the welfare workers in this country so that they may demand more money from the government and better administration of the welfare system of this country.

7. We call for $20,000,000 to establish a National Black Labor Strike and Defense Fund. This is necessary for the protection of black workers and their families who are fighting racist working conditions in this country.

*8. We call for the establishment of the International Black Appeal (IBA). This International Black Appeal will be

*(Revised and approved by Steering Committee)

funded with no less than $20,000,000. The IBA is charged with producing more capital for the establishment of cooperative businesses in the United States and in Africa, our Motherland. The International Black Appeal is one of the most important demands that we are making for we know that it can generate and raise funds throughout the United States and help our African brothers. The IBA is charged with three functions and shall be headed by James Forman:

    (a) Raising money for the program of the National Black Economic Development Conference.

    (b) The development of cooperatives in African countries and support of African Liberation movements.

    (c) Establishment of a Black Anti-Defamation League which will protect our African image.

9. We call for the establishment of a Black University to be funded with $130,000,000 to be located in the South. Negotiations are presently under way with a Southern University.

10. We demand that IFCO allocate all unused funds in the planning budget to implement the demands of this conference.

In order to win our demands we are aware that we will have to have massive suppport, therefore:

(1) We call upon all black people throughout the United States to consider themselves as members of the National Black Economic Development Conference and to act in unity to help force the racist white Christian churches and Jewish synagogues to implement these demands.

(2) We call upon all the concerned black people across the country to contact black workers, black women, black students and the black unemployed, community groups, welfare

organizations, teacher organizations, church leaders and organizations explaining how these demands are vital to the black community of the U.S. Pressure by whatever means necessary should be applied to the white power structure of the racist white Christian churches and Jewish synagogues. All black people should act boldly in confronting our white oppressors and demanding this modest reparation of 15 dollars per black man.

(3) Delegates and members of the National Black Economic Development Conference are urged to call press conferences in the cities and to attempt to get as many black organizations as possible to support the demands of the conference. The quick use of the press in the local areas will heighten the tension and these demands must be attempted to be won in a short period of time, although we are prepared for protracted and long range struggle.

(4) We call for the total disruption of selected church sponsored agencies operating anywhere in the U.S. and the world. Black workers, black women, black students and the black unemployed are encouraged to seize the offices, telephones, and printing apparatus of all church sponsored agencies and to hold these in trusteeship until our demands are met.

(5) We call upon all delegates and members of the National Black Economic Development Conferences to stage sit-in demonstrations at selected black and white churches. This is not to be interpreted as a continuation of the sit-in movement of the early sixties but we know that active confrontation inside white churches is possible and will strengthen the possibility of meeting our demands. Such confrontation can take the form of reading the Black Manifesto instead of a sermon or passing it out to church members. The principle of self-defense should be applied if attacked.

(6) On May 4, 1969 or a date thereafter, depending upon local conditions, we call upon black people to commence the disruption of the racist churches and synagogues throughout the United States.

(7) We call upon IFCO to serve as a central staff to coordinate the mandate of the conference and to reproduce and distribute en masse literature, leaflets, news items, press releases and other material.

(8) We call upon all delegates to find within the white community those forces which will work under the leadership of blacks to implement these demands by whatever means necessary. By taking such actions, white Americans will demonstrate concretely that they are willing to fight the white skin privilege and the white supremacy and racism which has forced us as black people to make these demands.

(9) We call upon all white Christians and Jews to practice patience, tolerance, understanding and nonviolence as they have encouraged, advised and demanded that we as black people should do throughout our entire enforced slavery in the United States. The true test of their faith and belief in the Cross and the words of the prophets will certainly be put to a test as we seek legitimate and extremely modest reparations for our role in developing the industrial base of the Western world through our slave labor. But we are no longer slaves, we are men and women, proud of our African heritage, determined to have our dignity.

(10) We are so proud of our African heritage and realize concretely that our struggle is not only to make revolution in the United States, but to protect our brothers and sisters in Africa and to help them rid themselves of racism, capitalism, and imperialism by whatever means necessary, including armed struggle. We are and must be willing to fight the defamation of our African image wherever it rears its ugly

head. We are therefore charging the Steering Committee to create a Black Anti-Defamation League to be funded by money raised from the International Black Appeal.

(11) We fully recognize that revolution in the United States and Africa, our Motherland, is more than a one dimensional operation. It will require the total integration of the political, economic, and military components and therefore, we call upon all our brothers and sisters who have acquired training and expertise in the fields of engineering, electronics, research, community organization, physics, biology, chemistry, mathematics, medicine, military science and warfare to assist the National Black Economic Development Conference in the implementation of its program.

(12) To implement these demands we must have a fearless leadership. We must have a leadership which is willing to battle the church establishment to implement these demands. To win our demands we will have to declare war on the white Christian churches and synagogues and this means we may have to fight the total government structure of this country. Let no one here think that these demands will be met by our mere stating them. For the sake of the churches and synagogues, we hope that they have the wisdom to understand that these demands are modest and reasonable. But if the white Christians and Jews are not willing to meet our demands through peace and good will, then we declare war and we are prepared to fight by whatever means necessary. . . . Brothers and sisters, we no longer are shuffling our feet and scratching our heads. We are tall, black and proud.

And we say to the white Christian churches and Jewish synagogues, to the government of this country and to all the white racist imperialists who compose it, there is only one thing left that you can do to further degrade black people and that is to kill us. But we have been dying too long for this country. We have died in every war. We are dying in Vietnam today fighting the wrong enemy.

The new black man wants to live and to live means that we must not become static or merely believe in self-defense. We must boldly go out and attack the white Western world at its power centers. The white Christian churches are another form of government in this country and they are used by the government of this country to exploit the people of Latin America, Asia and Africa, but the day is soon coming to an end. Therefore, brothers and sisters, the demands we make upon the white Christian churches and the Jewish synagogues are small demands. They represent 15 dollars per black person in these United States. We can legitimately demand this from the church power structure. We must demand more from the United States Government.

But to win our demands from the church which is linked up with the United States Government, we must not forget that it will ultimately be by force and power that we will win.

We are not threatening the churches. We are saying that we know the churches came with the military might of the colonizers and have been sustained by the military might of the colonizers. Hence, if the churches in colonial territories were established by military might, we know deep within our hearts that we must be prepared to use force to get our demands. We are not saying that this is the road we want to take. It is not, but let us be very clear that we are not opposed to force and we are not opposed to violence. We were captured in Africa by violence. We were kept in bondage and political servitude and forced to work as slaves by the military machinery and the Christian church working hand in hand.

We recognize that in issuing this manifesto we must prepare for a long range educational campaign in all communities of this country, but we know that the Christian churches have contributed to our oppression in white America. We do not intend to abuse our black brothers and sisters in black churches who have uncritically accepted Christianity. We want them to understand how the racist white Christian church with its hypocritical declarations and doctrines of brotherhood has abused our trust and faith. An attack on the religious beliefs of black people is not our major objective, even though we know that we were not Christians when we were brought to this country, but that Christianity was used to help enslave us. Our objective in issuing this Manifesto is to force the racist white Christian church to begin the payment of reparations which are due to all black people, not only by the Church but also by private business and the U.S. government. We see this focus on the Christian church as an effort around which all black people can unite.

Our demands are negotiable, but they cannot be minimized, they can only be increased and the Church is asked to come up with larger sums of money than we are asking. Our slogans are:

ALL ROADS MUST LEAD TO REVOLUTION
UNITE WITH WHOMEVER YOU CAN UNITE
NEUTRALIZE WHEREVER POSSIBLE
FIGHT OUR ENEMIES RELENTLESSLY
VICTORY TO THE PEOPLE
LIFE AND GOOD HEALTH TO MANKIND
RESISTANCE TO DOMINATION BY THE WHITE CHRISTIAN
    CHURCHES AND THE JEWISH SYNAGOGUES
REVOLUTIONARY BLACK POWER
WE SHALL WIN WITHOUT A DOUBT

Appendix B*

West German Reparations to Nazi Victims

*From Nehemiah Robinson, *Ten Years of German Indemnification* (Conference on Jewish Material Claims Against Germany, New York, 1964), pp. 28–36, 39–41, 45–47.

The Federal Compensation Law [of 1956, also known as the BEG, an abbreviation for *Bundesentschädigungsgesetz*] showed many improvements over the preceding law. First, its validity was extended to the whole of Germany within the borders which existed on December 31, 1937, with one exception, while the preceding law dealt only with the Federal Republic and West Berlin, East Berlin being covered, as stated, by the Berlin Compensation Law. Thus, persecutees from German areas outside the Federal Republic became eligible. Some benefits were increased, such as certain annuities for loss of life. The minimum disability for eligibility to an annuity was decreased from 30% to 25% and the probability of the causal nexus between persecution and damage to health was declared as sufficient. The responsibility of the German Federal Republic (legally of the Third Reich) for incarceration, and of other damage caused by foreign governments, was specifically stated. The notion of damage to liberty was expanded to include illegal life under inhuman conditions and the wearing of the Star of David everywhere. Maximum benefits granted for damage to property and professions were raised and compensation for the payment of discriminatory taxes was freed of ceiling restrictions. Considerable improvements were achieved in the field of compensation for professional damage: the maximum amount was raised, annuities were also introduced for former nonself-employed persons, the election of an annuity was made easier, the maximum monthly amount was increased, widows became eligible, and the inheritability of benefits under the Law was expanded in certain respects.

Some improvements were also introduced in the case of expellees, and stateless persons and refugees: in the case of expellees, fixed amounts for damage to professions were introduced, and widows became eligible for annuities. In the case of refugees and stateless persons, the cuts in the compensation amounts were eliminated; the prerequisite of deprivation of liberty was dropped. Only the period of initial annuity payments and some other differences remained unchanged.

The existing restrictions on payments were eliminated, with the exception of certain amounts above DM [German marks] 10,000, but even these became fully payable as of April 1, 1957.

The implementary regulations (the first three dealt with loss of life, damage to health, and damage to professions) were revised, and in some instances they expanded benefits of the Law, e.g., by permitting the accounting of income in foreign funds at a lower rate than at the official exchange rate or by introducing increases in the annuities for former employees.

The Implementation of the Legislation

The Extent of Implementation

The extent and general import of the law become evident from the data given below.

The two laws are statistically separated, except for the amounts paid out. In the latter respect, the statistics deal with the whole period as a unit; as regards filing and adjudication, the two periods are separated. Thus, to obtain a picture of the results of the implementation of the compensation legislation, one must treat the two periods separately.

During the effective period of the Federal Supplementary Law a total of 1,354,586 claims were on file. They consisted of those which were received on the basis of the Laender laws, as well as those filed after October 1, 1953. Due to time limitations, etc., not all claims were classified according to the residence of the claimant; thus, the 657,585 claims filed with the Compensation Agencies by foreign residents and the 530,295 by German residents represented part of the respective claims only. During that period, decision on 272,088 claims in toto and 63,739 in part were reached. Of those decided in toto 124,852 were positive. The total sum paid out during this period amounted to DM 1,062,153,000; of this total, DM 523,389,000 were paid to foreign and DM 538,-764,000 to German residents. Under the law a court claim is permitted against the adjudication by the Compensation Agency. During the validity of the first law, court suits were filed in 74,233 cases; in 52,483 cases decisions by the Court were reached. A part of the claimants, whose suits were rejected, appealed from these decisions to higher courts. . . .

In the second period, the compensation agencies' statistics encompass the claims which remained on file on June 30,

1956 and those filed thereafter. Although a filing deadline of April 1, 1958 was fixed in the law, it applied only to the initial filing, i.e., the submission of an application. Once the application was filed in time for any claim, the applicant has been permitted to register additional claims. This subsequent filing went on during the whole period. For instance, in 1959, over 130,000 new claims were registered with the Compensation Agencies. The year 1960 witnessed a considerable drop but in 1962 new claims almost reached the 100,000 mark.

Under the Federal Compensation Law, 2,976,140 claims were filed and registered in the above sense with the Compensation Agencies, 790,364 by residents of Germany and 2,185,776 by residents abroad. Of them, 2,489,396 were adjudicated by the Compensation Agencies: 732,686 filed by German residents and 1,756,710 by foreign residents. Not all claims were, however, dealt with in substance: 147,983 claims by German residents and 391,943 by foreign residents were disposed of otherwise than by award or rejection: they were, mostly, duplicate and triplicate claims filed under the Laender law, the 1953 law and 1956 law, claims withdrawn by the applicants, and claims without foundation in the law. Thus, a total of 1,949,470 claims were adjudicated on their merits; 584,703 by German and 1,364,767 by foreign residents. As a result of the adjudication by the Compensation Agencies there remained on file in these agencies, as of September 30, 1963, a total of 486,744 or some 16% of the total filed. Almost all of them (429,066) were by applicants residing abroad. The much higher ratio of adjudicated claims filed by German residents is mainly due to the circumstance that their adjudication started earlier and was frequently simpler, due to the geographical proximity. It ought to be mentioned that of the 486,744 claims on file, 213,062 or roughly 44%

were in Rheinland-Pfalz. Berlin still has 117,083 and Nord-
rhein-Westfalen 57,070 claims on file in the Compensation
Agencies. Of the rest only Bavaria had over 20,000 claims
each for local residents and foreign residents. . . .

A considerable part of the adjudicated claims was rejected by the Compensation Agencies: 283,262 filed by
German and 395,068 filed by foreign residents. Consequently, the total number of claims on which positive
awards were rendered by the Compensation Agencies was
1,271,140: 301,441 filed by German and 969,699 by foreign
residents. The ratio of claims recognized, in full or in
part, to those adjudicated by the Compensation Agencies
is almost exactly 1:2. The ratio is somewhat lower regard-
ing claims filed by German residents and somewhat
higher concerning claims by foreign residents. The basic
reason lies in the by far larger number of claims for deprivation of liberty filed by foreign residents. In this category the ratio of recognized claims to those adjudicated is
higher than the average and higher than for the same
category of claims by German residents.

The same is true of claims for professional damage;
307,850 court suits were filed with the courts of original
jurisdiction and 46,106 appeals were lodged with courts of
the secondary jurisdiction and in 2,208 instances with the
Supreme Court. In the first two court instances a number of
claims, rejected by the Compensation agencies, were recognized. For instance, the courts of original jurisdiction ruled
positively on 26,936 suits; in 75,916 cases amicable settlements were effected in court. A part of the positive decisions
was nullified on appeal by the competent Land; but in a
portion of the cases which was rejected by the court of original jurisdiction, positive decisions were reached in the courts
of secondary jurisdiction. During these ten years, DM 14,-

681,170,000 was paid out: DM 3,291,552,000 to residents of Germany and 11,389,618,000 to foreign residents. Since some of the claims granted provide not onetime payments but annuities, the value of the claims positively adjudicated will be higher than the amount cited. The Ministry of Finance estimates the present annual outlay for the recurrent annuities at DM 700 million and assumes that it will rise somewhat in the near future as more annuities will be granted. On the other hand, due to the natural death of recipients, some annuities are being discontinued and after a while the annual amounts will decrease progressively.

The largest single amount (DM 4,757,003,000–not counting advances) was paid for damage to professions (of it DM 3,888,233,000 to foreign residents). The second largest amount was for damage to health (DM 4,354,738,000; of it DM 3,130,019,000 went to foreign residents); the third largest was for damage to liberty (DM 2,375,171,000; of it DM 2,-193,770,000 went to foreign residents). For loss of life, DM 1,573,325,000 was paid; of it DM 1,149,640,000 went to foreign residents. . . .

The statistics are organized on the basis of claims, a claim representing a demand for compensation in any of the existing categories of damage (liberty, life, health, profession, etc.). There are no statistical figures on the number of applicants either in general, according to residence (in Germany or abroad) or otherwise. The number of claims filed does not represent the number of applicants: an applicant may have one or more claims, such as for deprivation of liberty, and at the same time for damage to health, and/or loss of life, professional damage, or loss of property. The Central Statistical Office in Duesseldorf, where claimants are all registered, carries the names of over 1,700,000 applicants. This figure, however, reflects not the number of persecutees but only those who were registered either as principals or as successors in right. The statistics also do not show the number of successful applicants, but only the number of claims positively adjudicated. The positive category includes every award, however small. Thus, for instance, the number of recipients of health annuities is much smaller than the number of positive awards for damage to health: frequently compensation is paid for a restricted period or only medical care is provided.

Although the law is a federal statute, its implementation is within the exclusive competence of the Laender, except for the enabling regulations for whose issuance the Federal Government has received special powers. Thus, the claims are filed with and adjudicated by Laender Compensation Agencies; court suits are filed with the ordinary courts and adjudicated by special chambers. . . .

Complications in Implementing the Law

The law is complicated and deals with events for which no precedents worth while existed. As mentioned, it is administered separately by each Land, the Federal Government having no powers over the administration. The costs of the program are shared by the Federal Government and the Laender fifty-fifty, except for Berlin, where the costs are shared by the Federal Government, the Laender and the City. In practice, the Federal Government carries 55% and all the Laender together 45% of the total costs. It was quite unavoidable that the implementation of such a law on separate bases would create difficulties of a legal and practical nature. The fact that the Supreme Court has to render almost

2,000 decisions is in itself an indication of the legal complexities. There is hardly any major provision of the law which, in one way or another, did not become controversial. The German authorities, the Claims Conference and the United Restitution Organization have invested innumerable efforts in making the law work, but there still are many unsolved problems.

Although a considerable number of claims—as shown above—were filed under the supplementary law of October, 1953, the processing, except for the Laender of the U.S. Zone and Berlin, was comparatively not large due to the need of establishing the apparatus, hiring of personnel, getting acquainted with the law and procedure, enactment of enabling regulations by the Federal and the Laender governments, etc. It took almost a year until the first enabling regulation (concerning claims for loss of life) was published on September 17, 1954; the second regulation (*re* damage to health) was published on December 25, 1954; the third regulation (*re* professional damage) on April 6, 1955 and the one providing for priorities in payments on February 22, 1955. The law contained only basic rules which had to be spelled out in the enabling regulations, so that the delay in their enactment of necessity provoked delays in adjudication. Several basic problems arose in the practice, in addition to those which were due to the brevity of the law and the lack of experience. Most prominent among them was the problem of liability under the law for persecutory measures by foreign governments, mostly those which were allied with the Third Reich (Japan, Rumania, Hungary, Bulgaria, Italy, Vichy France, Croatia), and in the case of some neutral countries, with regard to internment. Another problem which arose was that of the "residence quality" in a concentration camp or in a DP camp after the end of the war, a problem decided positively by the courts contrary to the view of the administrative agencies. The problems of who is an "expellee" and who is a "refugee," when and to whom hardship payments are to be made, were also among the problems in dispute. . . .

Damage to Health   No less difficulties have been encountered in the adjudication of claims for damage to health. The basic difficulties lie in the proof of the causal nexus between the state of health (or, rather the loss of health) at the time of the medical examination and the time when the persecutory measures were applied; the nexus is required for the recognition of compensation. Neither the presumption of the existence of a causal nexus between certain acts of persecution and the damage to health as evidenced at the time of persecution or soon thereafter, nor the rule that the probability of the existence of a causal nexus suffices (introduced in 1956), proved satisfactory to deal with the results of persecutory acts which had occured 15 to 20 years earlier. The legal relevance of the aggravation of illnesses existing at the time of persecution by acts of persecution, the impact of the passage of time on once proven disability due to persecution, and a number of other problems of health cases were the subject of several decisions by the highest court, which until now have not been fully adhered to, in particular as regards cases settled beforehand. The problem of the medical examination of persons residing outside of Germany and of confirming the findings of the local "trusted physicians" (Vertrauensaerzte) has not yet found a proper solution. After long stretched-out interventions, German physicians were dispatched to New York, to examine the findings on the spot. The necessary complement of physicians was rarely present, however, and an extension of the program to other overseas localities could not be achieved.

The fact that claimants were classified by the law into four particular categories, depending upon the group of officials competent to fix the amount of compensation, the fixing of the percentage of incapacity in each case and of the annuity due, have also provided innumerable road-blocks in the way of a smooth adjudication of claims for damage to health.

Damage to Professions   Here, too, the problems of application and interpretation have been many and complicated. Several remain outstanding. First is the definition of "satisfactory income" as such (this is the basis on which a decision whether an annuity is due or not depends); second is the conversion rate (to convert the income received in a foreign currency into German marks); third is the start of the annuity (after many annuities had been granted, the Supreme Court decided on a much less advanced starting point, not justified by either The Hague Protocol or the working of the law, thus creating an inequality between the same groups of persecutees); fourth is the right to elect an annuity, in particular by widows and other survivors. These have been the basic problems to be faced, in addition to some problems peculiar to certain countries (Israel, and the U.S.A., for instance).

Differences in the rules of compensation between self-employed persons and those not self-employed, the problem of which income is to be set off and which not have also slowed down adjudication and frequently led to unwarranted rejections of claims.

Loss of Life   The requirement in the law calling for proof in many instances as a precondition for granting annuities to survivors that the persecutee who lost his life supported or would have supported the survivor, caused problems and difficulties which have not been solved, for the most part. The difficulties are aggravated where the survivor had a number of relatives who had supported him or would have had to do so. . . .

The Government Bill to Amend the BEG

The need to amend the 1956 law has been evident for very long; preparatory work by a special committee has been going on for some time. However, it was only in July, 1963, that a formal government bill was passed by the Cabinet and presented to the Upper House (Bundesrat) which, having considered it in its first reading, sent it back to the Cabinet for further action, together with a few amending proposals. . . . *

The bill, as submitted, contains 106 specific amendment proposals, not counting the transitory provisions, and three new chapters. Many of them are more or less technical in nature, intended to clarify the existing text without involving basic changes. There are also a number of substantive changes, not all of them improvements, unfortunately. The bill contains a number of provisions designed to eliminate or curtail rights existing under the wording of the 1956 law and/or its interpretation by the Supreme Court.

Basically, the improvements consist of: a) a direct adaptation (and in some instances, newly introduced) of the amounts of annuities to the increase in the salaries of officials; b) some improvements in the granting of annuities to survivors for damage to professions; c) an increase in the amount of compensation for interruption of education; d) the

*The bill was enacted, substantially as described above.

provision of health care for victims of persecution residing in Germany, even though the illness was not due to persecutory measures; e) the provision of some compensation for damage to professions, by way of hardship, to residents of Germany not otherwise eligible thereto; f) an adaptation of earlier decisions in health and professional damage to the new administrative or judicial practices; g) the introduction of a presumption that a 25% incapacity of persecutees, who spent at least one year in a concentration camp, was due to persecution, if the general incapacity is at least as high; in addition, hardship payments may be provided for damage to health if uncertainty exists in medical science on the probability of the causal nexus between persecution and damage to health; h) the inhabitants of the City of Danzig are to be treated equally with those of the Reich.

The bill also introduces some improvements in the case of former residents of Germany dwelling outside the present area of the Federal Republic, but who did not emigrate during the Nazi period. Some improvements in favor of the "national" persecutees were also introduced in accordance with the 1960 Agreement with the High Commissioner for Refugees. A fund of DM 600 million is proposed for persecutees who are not eligible under the present law and are also not nationals of a country with which a global agreement has been concluded. Beneficiaries would basically be the post-1953 refugees and some smaller groups. The payments are not to be a matter of right but only "hardship payments." Eligible are to be non-remarried widows of persecutees who were deprived of liberty for at least one year, provided they do not reside in a country whence Germans were expelled or in East Germany or in East Berlin. The amounts and modalities of payment are to be laid down in a special regulation.

The bill also contains some procedural improvements, for instance, some extension of the admissibility of legal appeals. It sets a time-limit to claims (when an application had been submitted in time), which does not exist under the law.

The Government put a DM 3 billion valuation on the amendments. The estimates for the various proposals (except the fund and the increase in the compensation for damage to education) are not known.

Acknowledgments

This book, whose genesis is described at the beginning of Chapter 1, is a revised and expanded version of two lectures I gave at Ohio State University in January 1971 in the College of Law's Law Forum series. I am indebted to the dean and members of the Ohio State law faculty for their hospitality on that occasion. I am also grateful to John Gearin and Mark Tushnet for imaginative research assistance, to Otto Kuester for his hospitality in Stuttgart in 1969, when I was studying the German reparations program that owes so much to his persistent support, to Kenneth Kaufman for editorial aid, and to Marie Neuse for typing an inordinate mass of manuscript for so short a book.

B. I. B.